T0129849

The Story of You

*God's Plan to Save You
and Everybody Else*

S.E. Hicko

authorHOUSE®

AuthorHouse™
1663 Liberty Drive
Bloomington, IN 47403
www.authorhouse.com
Phone: 1 (800) 839-8640

Published by AuthorHouse 10/25/2018

ISBN: 978-1-5462-6594-8 (sc)
ISBN: 978-1-5462-6592-4 (hc)
ISBN: 978-1-5462-6593-1 (e)

CONTENTS

INTRODUCTION

The Good News

Do you have a loved one who has died without Jesus? He or she had problems and never really overcame their sin. They died without believing in the goodness of God. They never accepted Jesus as their personal lord and savior and certainly never got baptized. Where does religion say your loved is right now? Burning in eternal hell? Separated from God forever with no chance of salvation? My goodness, the limits and sickness that religion puts on God is mind blowing. I hope you don't believe this nonsense. I'm here to tell you that Christians and religion have lied to you. This is not wishful thinking as scripture attests: that as surely as your loved one is dead, he or she will be saved and with God forever. **God is the Savior of all men, especially those that believe (1 Timothy 4:10).**

God's love, according to religion, is limited, weak and conditional. God only loves you if you do or believe certain things and that love runs out if you die before you figure it out. Muslims and Jews believe that God will torture people for all eternity. Christians believe that God will burn people forever as well. Every religion on earth is focused on the human as the deciding factor as to eternal destiny. Christianity for example, claims that Jesus died for sin but the deciding factor of a hellish or heavenly destiny is squarely on whether or not a person believes this message or performs certain works. According to these religions, some will make it and some will not. God's love runs out on people that do not toe the line. After all, if a person is burning and kept alive through this conscious suffering for all eternity, then that love has without doubt, ran out.

Christians want to quote John 3:16, **for thus God loves the world, so that He gives His only-begotten Son, that everyone who is believing in Him should not be perishing, but may be having life eonian.** But according to these religious folk, that love of God runs out on people. If a person does not believe, does not get baptized, commits certain sins, doesn't perform sacraments or any combination of these things, then Jesus's death does not apply to them and hell or eternal separation awaits them. Therefore, depending on what denomination you belong to, a person must continually be in the right standing with God in order to be saved. What happens if your belief wavers or you can't overcome specific sins in your life? You're out!

Therefore, salvation is not a sure thing and is dependent on human action. This means nothing is certain and you could lose your standing with God at any moment because of your behavior. For me, this type of conditional love presented by the church is a farce! Believe in my son or I will burn you forever is a sick, vindictive lie created by religion in order to control people and get the offerings flowing to the church. God is not a bipolar, schizophrenic sociopath that loves you one moment and then pulls the rug out from you and tortures you forever if you fail. How can anyone trust in a god like that? Thankfully, this is not the true God of scripture.

A woman asks a man: "Will you still love me in the morning," when the man is courting her. The woman wants to know if the man will still love her when she is not as attractive and things become more difficult. Personally, the only love I can trust in is one in which God loves enough to still love me even at my worst. The love worthy of God is strong enough to love me even if I die in sin and unbelief. Even if I hate God, He will still love me. That's the certainty of love that I need and thankfully, that is exactly the love that God has not only for me, but for all of us! God's love never fails. **Christ Jesus came into the world to save sinners (1 Timothy 1: 15-16)** not those that respond to Him properly or follow religious rules. We all are sinners and Jesus saves us even while we are at our worst. He saves us even if we die without believing in Him. Jesus saves even the vilest sinner that has never repented. He loves us when we are unlovable.

The Apostle Paul, in chapter 5 of Romans, says that **while we are still sinners, Christ died for our sakes. For if, being enemies, we were conciliated to God through the death of His Son, much rather, being conciliated, we shall be saved in His life (Romans 5: 10-11).** The bible says that Christ made things right with us WHILE WE WERE ENEMIES! God does not make us perform or believe for Him in order to save us. Instead, through the death of Jesus, God makes things right with those that are enemies. This is a huge and overlooked message of the love of God. This scripture tells us that Christ has made things right between God and humans before the humans did anything to please God. He conciliated us WHILE WE WERE ENEMIES.

We are all enemies of God at some point as scripture says **For God**

has bound everyone over to disobedience so that He may have mercy on them all (Romans 11:32). Jesus takes care of all sins as attested in scripture. **He (Jesus) is the atoning sacrifice for our sins and not only for ours but also for the sins of the whole world (1 John 2:2).** Just as sure as death comes to all people and we experience it, so shall everlasting life come to all people and every last one of us will experience it (1 Corinthians 15:22). You see, Christ's death saved every man, woman and child that has ever walked the face of the earth. However, not everyone realizes it. In fact, most people do not realize it because they can't.

The god (Satan) of this age has blinded the minds of unbelievers so that they cannot see the light of the gospel of the glory of Christ, Who is the image of God (2 Corinthians 4:4). Satan has used religion and its puppets to convince people that God only loves you if you come to the altar or otherwise perform for Him. Church leaders twist the scripture to fit their bogus doctrines and push it on unsuspecting, trusting individuals. This is brainwashing in the worst form. Religion teaches that Christ's death and God's love are dependent upon and only work if humans contribute belief or works. If they don't contribute, then people forfeit the death and resurrection and consequently, God's love. Please! That is Satan's teaching if ever I heard it. Don't believe it! Humans do not have the power to overcome or thwart the death and resurrection of Jesus Christ nor the love of God.

The church, religion and Satan have misrepresented Jesus Christ and God in the worst way. Because of this, many believe that God will torture people forever and has no sovereign power or desire to ever rescue this part of creation. The lies of eternal hell, man's free-will and the teaching that the dead are not dead are taught in mainstream religion and society. It is difficult to break free from these chains but God has given faith and a realization of the truth to some people. These people that believe that Jesus died and will eventually save all mankind through His death and resurrection will have the privilege of ruling and reigning with Christ. They will have a special salvation. These people come in early to knowledge of the truth because God gave them the grace and faith to believe. True believers did not earn or deserve this but instead God chose them. **For it is by grace you have been saved through faith, and this is not from** yourselves, it is the gift of God—not by works, so that no one can boast (Ephesians 2: 8-10).

God, Who saves us and calls us with a holy calling, not in accord with acts, but in accord with His own purpose and the grace which is given to us in Christ Jesus before the beginning of time (2 Timothy 1:9). God chose the people that would believe this message before the beginning of time, before they were even born. It is God's choice to give belief to and save a select few now. The rest of humanity, He will save later. So if your loved one missed the boat or did not come to Jesus in this life; the death and resurrection of Christ Jesus still saves him or her. They will go through judgement and this is never pleasant, however, **when God's judgements come upon the earth, the people of the world learn righteousness (Isaiah 26:9).**

The title of this book is "The Story of You" because I want you to know that God has a unique and individual plan custom made for you and only you. It is true that all people will be with God because of the death and resurrection of Christ Jesus. These righteous actions of God's Son will save everyone. However, each will be saved in their own order (1 Corinthians 15:23). Also, each will go through their own set of evil and pain in this life. This evil and pain is given to you specifically by God to shape, teach and prepare you for the future joy of God dwelling in you. God states in Isaiah 45:7, **"I create evil."** He also **created your inmost being and knit you together in your mother's womb (Psalm 139:13).** Your pain, struggles, failures and sin are all a part of God's creative process. He is shaping you for immortality and an eternal destiny that can only be fully enjoyed because of the unique evil and pain that you endured. The joy will be that much greater because you endured so much pain. **You are God's workmanship (Ephesians 2:10)** and your heart will be throbbing with joy forever!

Your eternal destiny is set and unchangeable. You will not remain dead but will be resurrected to eternal bliss because of Jesus Christ. This fact can never change. You can never do anything to lose your place in heaven because your place in heaven was never based on anything you did or didn't do. Your place in heaven is based on Jesus Christ and what He did! Christ Jesus's death and resurrection applies to you whether you accept it or not. Now, God does give some people a realization of this truth now. These people are members of a body that Jesus will one day use to help bring the rest of humanity to a place that realizes this truth. It is wonderful if God gives you the faith to realize this now in this life. But, if not, He will give it to you at a later time. Your loved one that died without Jesus Christ will one day rise from the dead by the power of Jesus Christ. This will happen after death is destroyed; however, it will most definitely happen. God will one day dwell in everyone (1 Corinthians 15:28), for that is the glorious plan that fulfills and validates every evil that built up to this point.

This book was written over years of studying scripture and looking into the proper meanings of the words used. The purpose is to give my readers an introduction into the real truth of scripture that has been hidden by main stream society, Christianity and other religions. Pastors do not teach these truths because they come from institutions that have relied on lies for so long that they teach them as unquestionable truths. Of course, I encourage you to look and study scripture for yourself. The more you study these truths the more they will become evident to you. It is my prayer that you search out the truth and put any religious or societal preconceived notions on the shelf. Please look at the bible through what the words actual say not what others tell you they say. You will see that every story and every verse in scripture taken in the right context, teaches that God loves all people and will save all people. I may be repetitive at times but the lies have been so entrenched in the individual's mind that driving the point home is very necessary.

"The story of you" is God's plan for your life. He has formed your being and has created your life and circumstances. God has planned every moment of your life down to the tiniest minutia of detail and leaves nothing to chance. Though there are some joys in this life, **it is an experience of evil God has given to the sons of humanity to humble them by it (Ecclesiastes 1: 13).** God does not waist any experience or pain that you go through. We don't know what will happen tomorrow and life unfolds for us moment by moment in a way we cannot know. This is how we live as humans; God, however, **declares the end from the beginning, from ancient times, what is still to come. God's purpose will stand and He will do all that He pleases (Isaiah 46:10).**

God has planned your life and the lives of your loved ones. He even planned the failures and mistakes that you have made and the ones you will make in the future. However, God also sent his Son to be **slain from the foundation of the world (Revelation 13:8).** This means that God provided the answer to your sin and infirmities before you were even born. Christ Jesus will one day make every wrong right and the hole that evil and death has caused in your life will be filled completely. Your heart will throb with joy and the experience of life that God created you to walk in will lead you into perfection. Jesus will destroy sin, evil and death so all is left is life. Life filled with the glory of God for you and all your loved ones, no matter what happens!

CHAPTER 1

THE EARLY CHURCH TAUGHT THE TRUTH; TODAY'S CHURCH, NOT SO MUCH

Some may think that believing that Jesus Christ will save every man, woman and child that has ever or will ever walk the face of the earth is some fairy-tale, made-up, new age idea. Some may believe that eliminating the possibility of an eternal hell throws everything off balance. However, this book is written to show the truth of what the bible actually teaches.

In fact, if serious research is done, one would find that the belief that Jesus would save all mankind was the predominant belief in the early church. Theological schools in Alexandria, Antioch and other places taught this truth. Many church fathers, such as: Origen and Clement of Alexandria can be quoted clearly on their belief that Jesus would save all. These early church fathers spoke the Greek language in which the New Testament was written, so they knew the language and meaning well.

It wasn't till hundreds of years later, when the Romans got a hold of scripture, that words were mistranslated and corrupted. These government officials and church fathers did not speak the language of the New Testament Greek. Therefore, words that actually mean "age" or "ages" were translated to mean "eternal." Words that described physical locations like "Gehenna," a valley just outside of Jerusalem or "the grave, unseen" were translated to mean "hell."

The Roman government and church leaders chose to control the masses using fear and the threat of eternal torment, so they manipulated the scripture to fit their agenda. As a result, years of tradition have sprung from this deceit and now these heresies are believed as unquestionable truths.

We need to explore what the bible actually teaches. We need to know that the devil is not the enemy at the gate, but that he has invaded the church thousands of years ago and is disguised as an angel of light and his ministers as servants of righteousness. I think it is important to understand that just because it seems like evil is running rampant, that God is still in control of it, and Satan can do nothing apart from the sovereign God. Likewise, no human being can act independently of their creator using supposed 'free-will.' God is the source and cause of all things as scripture would attest.

I believe that if we look at the Holy Scriptures without the lens of false translation and tradition, to seek the truth of what is actually said, we will know that God would not devise a plan in which most of his creation would end up in an eternal hell. However, God is powerful enough and willing enough to devise a plan that would end with all of his creation present with him forever. I believe this is exactly what the bible teaches.

So, I pose the question, is everything you learned about God true? God is beyond the limits of my imagination and comprehension. His power and love are on levels that the human mind cannot fathom. However, within our human limits, it is important to try to understand all we can, to seek the truth of the Almighty.

Over the past years, I have had a revelation similar to the main character "Hiccup" in the Pixar movie <u>How to Train Your Dragon.</u> At a point in the movie, when Hiccup realizes that the dragons are not the evil beasts everyone has portrayed them as over the past 300 years, he says, "Everything we know about you guys is wrong." I have had a similar experience with what I have been taught about God through the church, Christians, religion, media and other sources. Everything I have been taught about God is wrong.

It is popular belief in Christianity that Jesus Christ died for our sins to reconcile us back to God (which is true) but humans need to accept this gift or make a free will choice to believe in Christ in order to go to heaven. If not, that person will go to hell. Christianity teaches that an outside source called the devil created evil and invaded God's precious, good creation. Is this True? I will discuss the Holy Scriptures and the support for the fact that humans do not possess free will, evil was created by God for a grand purpose, and that God will eventually save every human being. The premise is that we as humans all make choices; however, we cannot act independently of God.

Who is responsible for man's salvation? Ask any Christian, who is responsible for your salvation? They will respond, Jesus Christ! Okay then, Mr. Christian, who is responsible for an unbeliever going to hell? It is that man's choice to reject Jesus, so it is his own fault, says Mr. Christian. So, you need to be smart enough or spiritual enough to choose Christ? Yes, says Mr. Christian. Then, isn't it man who is responsible for his own salvation? No. It is all of God. Okay, if salvation is all of God, then not having salvation has to be all of God. Then isn't it all of God if someone goes to hell? If man has to choose Christ then the deciding factor of salvation is in man's control. This is human pride, that we decide our everlasting destiny. God is sovereign, He decides, and He alone is the master of our fate.

I often hear statements to the effect, "God is in Control" or "There is a reason for everything." Often these statements are made by well-meaning Christians, who in their next breath say that I must make a personal decision to accept Jesus Christ as my savior or I will not be saved. So I rationalize, if I have to make the ultimate choice, then how can God be in control at all, wouldn't I be in control? Maybe God could persuade or nudge me, but I had to make the ultimate decision to be saved. So again I rationalize, if it is up to me to make the most important decision of all, whether I accept Christ or not, then wouldn't the less important decisions fall into my lap as well. If I am in control of my endless destiny and given the free will to choose, then wouldn't I be entrusted with lesser decisions? Well then, how can God be in control at all? Also, if God is not in control of everything, then how can I trust him with anything?

These questions are important ones. If I need to rely on myself, others or some creator who is not in complete and total control, then how do I know that things won't spiral out of control in my life? I make mistakes all the time. In addition, if God defers his control to others, then how can I be assured that this world isn't just one big random chance?

The answer that scripture gives is that we, as humans, do not have free will and God is in complete control of our lives now and He is in complete control of our eternal destiny. Now, before everyone rushes at me and says, "What are you talking about, I make decisions every day and I do what I want!" I don't doubt that people make their own choices; we do it thousands of times every single day. But, scripture says that these decisions, even our wants, especially our circumstances are all under the influence and control of the Almighty God.

CHAPTER 2

ETERNAL HELL DOES NOT EXIST

Skittles are my son's favorite candy. I decided to test him one day on his love for me by using the small candies as bait. He was ten years old at the time and I left him in the house alone as I snuck out back. Before I left, I told him that he can eat any food in the house except for the package of Skittles that I left in the middle of the house on the kitchen table. If he ate of the Skittles left on the table, then he would be punished. I peered through the kitchen window as my son started walking up to the package of skittles on multiple occasions. Each time though, he refused the urge to eat the forbidden candy. Then, I saw my son's best friend sitting outside and asked him to come over. I paid the friend ten dollars to go in the house and test my son by convincing him to eat the skittles. He gladly accepted and was given entrance into the house after knocking on the front door.

"Wow! Look at those skittles," the friend exclaimed excitedly. Let's eat them he shouted. My son calmly explained that they could eat anything in the house except for the bag of skittles. Otherwise, he would be punished by his dad. The friend said, "Is that really what your dad said, will you really be punished?" The friend continued to chip away at my son's defenses and the urge to eat his favorite candy combined with his neighbors encouragement, became too much. My son ripped open the bag of skittles and ate. He gave some to his friend as well. As soon as I saw him eat, I jumped through the back door and said, "Why have you eaten of the skittles that I told you not to eat?" I angrily sent his friend home and banished my son to his bedroom where he would stay for the rest of his life. He died an eighty year old man, never once leaving his room.

Of course, the only truth to this story is that my son does like skittles. The rest is fictitious and completely ridiculous. But, I have a story that is even more ridiculous and even more untrue. It is the story that is told in religion today. It is a story of a loving God that would torture His children in flesh burning fire for all eternity because Adam and Eve ate a delicious piece of fruit. However, the reason why this story is such a believable lie is that, as religion skillfully always does, it contains some truth. For instance, God did put Adam and Eve in a situation in which they would fail. Also, this failure or sin did spread to all of creation though it was a part of God's plan from the very beginning. This will be discussed later in the book. Unfortunately, the true parts of the story lead to one of the greatest lies of all: The unscriptural lie that anyone, let alone most of creation will spend an eternity burning in hell.

Did you think punishing my son for the rest of his life for eating skittles was a ludicrous punishment? Well, how about Adam and Eve eating of the fruit? This was a sin committed by a finite human being that has eternal consequences? How about the people that were born after Adam? What about us today? We will sin because we inherited this sin and death from Adam. Therefore, all humanity is heading to eternal hell as a default at birth. This story is infinitely worse than me punishing my son and separating him from my presence for the rest of his life for eating skittles.

The truth, the full truth, is that God intended for Adam and Eve to sin and consequently bring sin and death to all humans. Then, through using sin and death, God will shape all humanity into His perfect creation. We will look into this more later. For now, it is important to not add words to scripture. The eternal hell as we know it does not exist anywhere in scripture. The consequence for man's sin was always and will always be death. **For the wages of sin is death…(Romans 6:23).** The wages of sin is not eternal torture, but death. We would remain dead if it were not for Jesus providing the way out through His suffering, death and resurrection. Jesus saves us from death because He experienced death for us. He did not experience eternal hell because it is not what He is saving us from.

So to play devil's advocate, I ask the question: When was hell created? **In the beginning Elohim created the heavens and the earth…(Genesis 1:1).** There is no mention of creating hell at any point throughout the scripture. The bible says that Jesus was slain since the foundation of the world in Revelations 13:8, so sin was already part of God's plan. Yet, God did not mention the eternal place of torcher. Then God created Adam and Eve and told them not to eat from the tree in the midst of the garden or they would go to ETERNAL HELL! This was perfect timing to threaten Adam and Eve with this awful fate so maybe they will listen to God. Wait a minute; this is not what God said. He said that if they ate from the tree then they would die. Adam and Eve touched the tree and ate from the tree. This is it, the first sin of mankind! What a great time for God to introduce the concept of eternal hell for sinners. However, eternal hell was not discussed, but like God said, Adam and Eve would die or begin to die when they ate of the fruit. DEATH, not eternal hell, is the destiny of all mankind because of the actions of Adam.

Okay, now I got it. God would certainly introduce the eternal hell concept after the first murder ever recorded. Cain and Abel were the offspring of Adam and Eve. Cain was angry that God accepted his brothers sacrifice over his, so he lured Abel to the field and proceeded to kill him. Cain took the life of his brother in a hot rage of jealousy. Now, God will speak to Cain about his future destiny in eternal hell. Indeed, God did speak to Cain: **Now you are cursed, away from the ground which has opened wide its mouth to take your brother's blood from your hand. When you serve the ground, it shall not continue to give its vigor to you. A rover and a wanderer shall you become on earth (Genesis 4: 11-12).**

In Genesis 4:13, Cain said to the Lord, "My punishment is too great for me to bear. This was Cain's response to God punishing him. How did God punish him? God punished Cain by not allowing the ground to yield crops for him anymore and making him a wanderer on the earth. If this was too much for Cain to bear then how is he going to respond to the knowledge that eternal hell awaits him? Well, the truth is that God never mentioned eternal hell because it does not exist and has never entered His mind. Eternal hell, if it were real, would have been introduced right from the start, don't you think? God never threatens anyone with this torment. Death is the enemy and the end result of man's mortality and sin, not hell. There is no passage of time or sensations in death and we would remain this way forever if it weren't for the death and resurrection of Jesus Christ. Jesus will one day destroy death for every last human being.

Follow the rest of the Old Testament and you will find no mention of the eternal hell that is taught in popular religion. Did you know that the apostle Paul, in his thirteen letters, never mentions hell at all, not even once! The book of Revelation mentions the Lake of Fire, but this is not hell and does not serve the purpose of the eternal hell taught by religion. The Old Testament uses the word 'Sheol' which simply means the 'grave or abode of the dead.' People go to the grave and are unseen when they die. This word 'Sheol' is translated in the bible to mean 'hell' but this simply is not the eternal hell of popular belief. They do not go to eternal hell but simply go to the grave. That's fine that the Old Testament does not threaten humanity with the eternal flames of hell or that the Apostle Paul doesn't mention it in the New Testament. It doesn't matter one might say, Jesus spoke on hell so it must be real. Well yes, the word hell is found in the four gospel accounts of the New Testament but that word does not mean what you think it does.

Jesus Christ did not speak English while He was on Earth. Therefore, His words have been translated in any given English bible. The word 'Hell' that is attributed to coming from the mouth of Christ has been translated from a Hebrew word 'Hinnom.' This is a location of a valley near Jerusalem. The word 'Gehenna' is the Greek word used in the gospel accounts and was derived from this Valley of Hinnom. Samuel G. Dawson sums up the origin of 'Gehenna' in his article Jesus' Teaching on Hell:

Gehenna, the name of a valley on the south and east of Jerusalem…which was so called from the cries of the little children who were thrown into the fiery arms of Moloch, i.e., of an idol having the form of a bull. The Jews so abhorred the place after these horrible sacrifices had been abolished by King Josiah(2 Kings 23:10), that they cast into it not only all manner of refuse, but even the dead bodies of animals and unburied criminals who had been executed. And since fires were always needed to consume the dead bodies, that the air might not become tainted by the putrefaction, it came to pass that the place was called Gehenna.

So, the word that Jesus actually used was Gehenna not hell. Gehenna was actually a physical place near Jerusalem where trash and the bodies of dead criminals were thrown. It has nothing to do with an eternal place of punishment. The people that Jesus spoke to would have known this because this place was used to sacrifice little children to idols such as Molech. Jesus was speaking of earthly punishments and death, just like the entire Old Testament punishments. Jesus was talking about a garbage dump in each of the twelve passages that he preaches on hell. This hell, rather Gehenna, is on the earth and physical. It is not under the earth or eternal. Jesus warned the Jewish people of this physical valley located near them. He never warned them of a place of eternal fire and torture.

God's destiny for humanity is to create sons and daughters? What about all those who will be in hell? Yes, the word "hell" exists in the bible but that is a gross mistranslation and it is simply not found in the original Hebrew and Greek scriptures. I encourage anyone to do a concordant, or any, word study on the word "hell" each time it is used in the bible. The most common words used for hell are "Sheol" in the Old Testament, "Gehenna" and "Hades" in the New Testament. The meanings for these words are as follows:

Sheol – Grave, pit or abode of the dead.

Hades – unseen

Gehenna – actually a physical location in Jesus' time. It is actually a valley south of Jerusalem.

These words have nothing to do with life after death and certainly do not refer to a place of eternal torment. The eternal torment deception entered the church through mistranslation and corrupt leadership. It is a lie that deceives millions and keeps perhaps even more at an arms distance from God. I would have to write page after page to fully explain how the word 'hell' crept and slithered its way into the bible. The mixture and influence of Greek Mythology and Ancient Egyptian folklore is where corrupt, religious leaders learned of hell. Then, they used the fear and deceit of hell on people so that they could control the masses. This has been passed down from generation to generation in nearly every religion. However, nothing, no teaching at all could be further from the truth of God and Jesus Christ than the teaching of eternal hell. This teaching of hell tarnishes the true love of God and makes him a sick, "love me or a will torture you forever," lunatic.

This false teaching of eternal hell, I believe, is the number one reason people run from religion. After all, how can humans fully trust a God that would torture most of his creation? The answer is: they cannot. But, the glorious truth is that God will not torture anyone in hell forever but will save each and every human being. The scriptures that support this truth are too numerous to count.

George Carlin, the late comedian, and a man I admired for speaking out against the corrupt elite who run our governments and world, once did a bit on how ridiculous religion is. He stood up in front of his audience and said that religion has actually convinced us of the most absurd thing in the world. I can't quote him word for word, but he told the audience that there is some creator high in the sky who wrote down a bunch of rules on stone tablets and commanded people to follow them. However, the comedian goes on the say, if we break these rules he will send us to a place where we will be tortured, humiliated, burned and we will be experiencing unimaginable pain and suffering, and we will be in this place for all eternity. But…..God loves us! When Mr. Carlin said these words the audience burst into laughter and applause.

Most Christians would condemn this comedian; however he and many like him see the absurdity of an all-loving, all-powerful god sending people to such a place as the eternal hell described. Many people do not believe in God because they cannot justify how He is portrayed as love and then creates the most terrifying place imaginable and then sends most of His creation there. Or, they look around the world and see starving children, murder and death that can make the world such a terrible place. This is the opposite of love unless, one day, God sets every wrong right, and makes the best possible everlasting good out of every evil, for each and every human being. He will!

Back to George Carlin, I respected this man very much because he looked, like many today, beyond the phoniness of today's world and exposed the elite agenda of corruption within our governments, corporations and media outlets of the world. I just wish he, and others, would be able to look past the curtain of phoniness and lies of religion to see the truth. George Carlin takes the god of religion for what he is, an absolute joke, but never bothered it seems, to find out the truth about God. There is little truth in religion, about as much truth as in our governments and television programs.

How can Christians and people of various faiths love a god that loves so conditionally? If you toe the line, the Christian god will love you and be there for you. But, if you don't believe the right way or do the right thing, this god will torture you forever. I trust God because I know He will bring me home and I don't need to perform for Him to stay on His good side. It may be a brutal process, but I know when it is all said and done, I will be a Son of God. This will happen because of God, not because of me.

Eternal Hell is the sickest of all lies; I don't know what else to say. God will judge, but His judgements are for the good of the person being judged, like a loving father disciplining his child. Judgements, though fierce, are a part of His love. Translated properly, not one person in scripture, including Jesus, even uttered the word hell. I encourage you to look up the Greek and Hebrew words that are improperly translated to mean hell and eternity in the bible. However, you have to want to believe the truth and shun the lies of religion that only seek to control you with fear of a lunatic god; the very reason hell was invented.

At any rate, do you have it in your heart to send people to an eternal hell? Does your pastor condemn people to eternal hell because they are not smart enough to believe as he does? Is your loved one in this God awful place? Is it possible that you will go there some day? Well, let me save the suspense. You can go there right now. The following is a picture of the hell that Jesus was talking about:

This is the valley of Gehenna that Jesus warned about. It is purely physical and you can go there today if you want to take a trip to Israel. Hell has nothing to do with yours or anyone else's eternal destiny! Jesus Christ saves us all and there is no such thing as eternal hell and there never was. Every part of God's creation will be with Him for all eternity because of Christ Jesus.

CHAPTER 3

DEAD PEOPLE ARE DEAD

I hate funerals. At funerals, people say stupid things. For example, "Look at Aunt May, she looks so beautiful and peaceful." Mind you that Aunt May is dead and in a coffin. But, people want to say that she looks great as a dead body? Then, I would hear people say, "Well Aunt May is alive in heaven looking down on us right now." I understand that people say things like this to comfort themselves and others because nobody likes death. However, do people really want to comfort themselves and others with pagan doctrines of false teachings just because it's easier to swallow? The truth is that Aunt May and all our loved ones that have died are dead and will not regain consciousness until resurrection day. We may not like death but it is part of the process that we must go through in order to put on immortality and everlasting life. Jesus went through death to show us the way home, through death. The resurrection is a big deal!

Eternal hell is the most disgusting fable ever told! But, Jesus is the savior of the world, the entire world. So we must ask: What does Jesus save us from if eternal hell is a farce? Well, Jesus saves us from sin and death. But, just what exactly is sin and death? This question and many others are actually answered in scripture. Let's first take a look at the Garden of Eden and the modern concept of sin and death:

Satan is the greatest liar of all time. He is a master of deceit because he includes as much truth in his lies as possible. God told Adam that **from every tree in the garden you may eat, yea eat. But from the tree of the knowledge of good and evil, you must not eat from it; for on the day you eat from it, to die you shall be dying (Genesis 2:16).** Notice that God told Adam this one and only rule before Eve was even created. Therefore, Eve would have received the knowledge of God's instruction from Adam. So Satan, right off the bat, attacks the one who would have received the word from another human, rather than straight from God. Otherwise, Satan would have started with Adam.

But the serpent said to the woman: Not to die shall you be dying; for God knows that on the day you eat of it your eyes will be unclosed, and you will become like God, knowing good and evil (Genesis 3: 4-5). Now, the knowing good and evil part of Satan's comment was actually true. In Genesis 3:22, **God said: Behold, man has become like one of Us in knowing good and evil.** The "knowing good and evil" part actually happened and is part of the process of God developing us into a perfect creation. Humans must have an experience of good and evil to have the contrast to fully enjoy the glory and goodness of God. However, the lie of Satan was delicately woven into the truth. The lie was that Adam and Eve would not die or begin to die once they ate of the fruit. Sadly today, religion continues to teach this lie of Satan within church walls.

Scripture says that **the wages of sin is death (Romans 6:23).** Christians simply do not believe in the scriptural definition of death as will be shown. **For the living know that they shall die, but the <u>dead know nothing whatsoever</u> (Ecclesiastes 9:5).** The bible says that the dead do not know anything. Popular religious and Christian belief is that a part of the soul lives on and goes to heaven or hell immediately upon death. Thus, these religions confirm and teach the lie of Satan that surely we will not die, but continue to live in some other realm. This lie diminishes the power of the resurrection and as we will soon see, causes people to deny the death and resurrection of Jesus Christ without even knowing it.

In the Old Testament death was very physical. The patriarchs died and went away. There was no mention of them or other humans living somewhere else after they died. Jesus spoke of Gehenna which was a physical location. The grave was referred to as a place people went after death where they were no longer seen. The bottom line: death is the absence and opposite of life. There is no feeling, sensations, passage of time or anything else in death as scripture says the dead know not anything. Death is not life for part of the soul in another form but is indeed death. Death may be a brutal, horrible process but being dead is like being in a deep sleep with no thoughts, emotions or anything else. You will make up at the resurrection and even if you were dead for 2,000 years it would feel as if you had just died. Jesus suffered, died and experienced the death state for us. God raised Him from the death state to show us how Jesus will one day raise us from the death state. Jesus is not snatching our soul back from heaven or hell at the resurrection to put us in some different body. He is raising us from the dead to have life. Then, at the Lord's appointed time, and only then, do we put on our immortality.

We need to digress and talk about the false doctrine of the 'Immortality of the soul' and then look at the true definition of the 'soul' from scripture. First, where does the belief that a soul goes to heaven or hell immediately after death come from? I am not going to get into too much detail about this but it can be traced back to ancient Egypt. Then from Egypt, the mythology of the soul living after death crept into Jewish and Greek thinking throughout the ages. As a result, religion and churches injected this belief into their doctrines. However, there is no scripture in the bible that teaches the immortality of the soul or that a part of a person lives on after death. The church simply mixed pagan doctrines from Egypt that ran down the pipe to their own cultures and accepted it as truth. Satan works in subtle ways. The immortality of the soul denies death, the very thing that Christ came to save us from. Not only that, the immortality of the soul denies the fact that Jesus ever died. One way Satan attacks the truth is by denying what Jesus did and what He saved humans from by redefining the word death to mean something it doesn't. If the soul lives on and humans don't actually die, then Jesus doesn't save us from death and He never actually died Himself.

This is not what scripture teaches at all. The Old Testament teaches that Adam died, Abraham died, Isaac died, Jacob died, Moses died and so on and so forth. There is no mention of any part of these people existing somewhere else after they died. Basically, they ceased to exist and have no thought, passage of time, or sensations at all as the dead know **nothing (Ecclesiastes 9:5)**. So what is life and death? Let's take a look at what scripture teaches about what the soul actually is.

God formed the human out of soil from the ground, and He blew into his nostrils the breath of life; and the human became a living soul (Genesis 2:7). Let's break this down. So God formed a body from the ground, it was a human body. Then, God blew the breath of life into the human and the human became a living soul. This teaches that the soul is the combination of a body and breath of life from God. The body was not alive; it had no feeling or self-realization when God formed it from the soil. Okay, God's next step was NOT to create a soul and put it in the human! No, His next step was to blow the breath of life into the body. The breath of life came out of God and into the body. Therefore, the fusion of the body and the breath of life became a living soul. The Hebrew word nephesh (5315) is the word used for soul. It is described as a soul, living being, life, self, person, desire, appetite, and emotion. The important point here is that the soul is not a separate part of a person that lives forever, rather a soul is formed when body and God's spirit come together.

The word nephesh is used many times in scripture when God was creating living beings. **And God said: Let the earth bring forth the living soul (nephesh), each according to its kind: domestic beast, creeper and land animal, each according to its kind (Genesis 1:24).** Some bible translations sub the word creature in for soul in this scripture. However, the Hebrew word used to describe all the creatures that God created, is nephesh, the same word meaning soul when God created the human. So in essence, all living creatures have a body and when that body is combined with God's spirit, they became a soul. They do not have a soul!

When God blew the breath of life into Adam's body, Adam had no consciousness or sensation when the breath was still with God. God formed a lifeless body and it was not until He breathed spirit into Adam that he became aware and alive. He became a living soul! A soul was not put into him. I'll repeat this hundreds of times because it is so important. If there is no body then the soul cannot exist, if there is not spirit or breath of life then the soul cannot exist. The soul is only formed when there is a body and God puts a spirit or breathes the breath of life into the body. The combination of the two is the soul.

So what happens when people die? **And the soil returns to the earth just as it was, and the spirit, it returns to the One, God, Who gave it (Ecclesiastes 12:7).** People die and their bodies are lifeless, they become part of the earth, rot and decay. The spirit (breath of life) of the person returns to God, Who gave it. Now this spirit is not an immortal soul that goes to heaven or hell. Remember, the soul or nephesh is the combination of body and spirit. At this point, the soul no longer exists and the spirit of the human goes back to God just as it was with God before He blew the breath of life into Adam. Adam had no consciousness or sensation until the moment God blew spirit into him, he was just a lifeless corpse. For those of us that die, the spirit leaves our body leaving it lifeless and the spirit goes to God just like Adam's spirit was the moment before God breathed life into him. We have no consciousness, thought or anything else when our spirit goes to God. **For the dead know nothing (Ecclesiastes 9:5).** This is death and we sin because we are going to die. This is the destiny of all humans and creatures on earth and this is what we must be saved from.

The following are some excerpts from the book of **Job chapter 14: 10-14:**

But a man dies and is laid low; he breathes his last and is no more

So he lies down and does not rise; till the heavens are no more, people will not awake

Or be roused from their sleep.

If someone dies will they live again? All the days of my hard service I will wait for my

Renewal to come.

There are many other verses is scripture that teach that the dead are dead. There are no verses in scripture that teach that humans or their soul go anywhere else but the grave when they die. The above selection in Job is one of many that relate death to sleep. In fact, this passage teaches that humans will not be raised or awakened from their sleep until the heavens are no more. We don't go anywhere when we sleep, we are unconscious. Death itself is a deep sleep and the bible does not leave any doubt about the teaching that no part of the human is alive anywhere else. Then, the million dollar question asked in **Job 14:14: If someone dies, will they live again?**

As I was driving up the highway to Michigan, I saw a giant billboard that read: If you died today, would you go to heaven or hell? This seems to be the question that religion asks. Little do they know that this question is blasphemy and contradicts the truth of the scripture. Simply put, it is the wrong question. The question that should be asked is in Job 14:14 that IF SOMEONE DIES, WILL THEY LIVE AGAIN? Death is the problem! We would remain dead forever and never rise from the grave if someone didn't save us from this fate. Death is what we need to be saved from, not eternal hell. IF SOMEONE DIES, WILL THEY LIVE AGAIN? YES, because Christ Jesus went to the grave and God raised Him from that grave. Christ will do the same for each one of us at our appointed time.

You see, the resurrection is a big deal. It is the answer to the problem of sin and death; in fact, it will destroy sin and death completely. The teaching of the 'Immortality of the soul' makes resurrection day unnecessary. If people or their souls are in heaven and hell immediately after they die, then what is the purpose of the resurrection? At resurrection, Christians would have us believe that souls are snatched from heaven and hell, given a new body at resurrection, and then returned to heaven and hell. That makes sense only to illogical, unscriptural based, religious minds. Nowhere in scripture is this taught. God said man would die and Satan lied about it. The church believes Satan and not God. The bible says the wages of sin is death. Moses died and went to the grave along with the patriarchs of the Old Testament. Jesus died and was in the dead state for three days. We all die and will be dead until the resurrection! This is serious because if one believes that Jesus's soul went somewhere else at His death than they are denying that Jesus actually died. This leads to another great lie of the Christian religion, THE TRINITY!

Satan is an evil genius because he tricks people into thinking they believe in Jesus when their own teachings actually deny Jesus. The trinity is one of those lies. Religion teaches that God is one in three parts, the Father, Son and Holy Ghost. This is not true as scripture would attest and not only that, but it denies the death and resurrection of Jesus Christ when you follow this teaching all the way through. First, from the mouth of Christ Himself: **I am going, and I am coming to you. If you loved Me, you would have rejoiced that I am going to the Father, for the Father is greater than I (John 14:28).**

If one is greater than the other, then they are not equal. No sense in getting into a squabble over who is greater, God or Jesus but these words from Jesus indicate that they are not the same being. Jesus is God's son and He has all the attributes of His Father but He is not His Father. When we look at Jesus, the full representation of God is seen. However, God and Jesus are not two equal parts of the same being. In fact, Jesus Christ actually will give up His reign and subject Himself completely to God. How many times have you heard that? Yes, Jesus will give up His reign and subject Himself to God at the appointed time. When will Jesus give up His reign? Jesus will give up His reign after He destroys death and saves the last human being and the last bit of creation. Christ Jesus will raise every man, woman and child from the dead and give them immortality along with the rest of creation. At that point, Jesus hands over the entire creation that He saved, including Himself, to God so that He will be all things to all creation. Don't believe me? Here are the scriptures that prove it.

Thereafter the consummation, whenever He (Jesus) may be giving up the kingdom to His God and Father, whenever He should be nullifying all sovereignty and all authority and power. <u>For He must be reigning UNTIL He should be placing all enemies under His feet.</u> The last enemy is being abolished: death (1 Corinthians 15: 24-27).

The above scripture shows that Christ will reign <u>until</u> He puts all enemies under His feet. This word 'until' means that at this point in God's plan, Jesus ends His rule and completes His mission of destroying death and saving all creation. Jesus gives up His rule and presents His accomplished work to God, His Father, NOT to Himself. Then, the bible goes on to say that Jesus will subject Himself to God so that God will be all in all. Notice it does not say that Jesus subjects Himself to Himself but to God. Clearly, there are different roles between Jesus and God. Jesus and God are not one. They may be one in purpose but not in being. God is Jesus's Father. Jesus is the Son of God as the bible says over and over.

For He subjects all under His feet. Now whenever He may be saying that all is subject, it is evident that it is outside of Him Who subjects all to Him. Now, whenever all may be subjected to Him, <u>then the Son Himself also shall be subjected to Him Who subjects all to Him,</u> that God may be All in all (1 Corinthians 15: 27-28).

Jesus will be subjected to God once He fulfills His mission of saving all creation. He is a separate entity from God but always follows the will of God and is the perfect manifestation of the Father. In this way, they are one. However, they are not one being. The trinity denies the work of Christ because if you follow the teaching all the way through then Jesus did not actually die on the cross. The trinity says that Jesus's body died but that He was still alive in the form of the Father. If this is the case then Jesus never experienced the death state for us and is not our savior. This is how subtle tricks from the devil get religious people to think they believe in the truth but deny it with their own false teaching. However, Jesus did die; both His body and being, and God raised Him from the dead. Jesus was dead like we will one day be dead. So, we will rise as He rose because of His death. We will follow Him in death and then follow Him in resurrection. Jesus is our Savior that suffered and died for us!

Now, if God is not a trinity then what is He actually doing with respect to His Son? The truth is that God is expanding His family to have many sons and daughters just like Jesus! God will give immortal, blissful life to all of His creation through the suffering, death and resurrection of His Son, Jesus. However, Jesus saves some before others. This is all a part of God's will and foreknowledge. God chooses to conform people to the image of His Son so that these people will become His very sons and daughters. This is an expanding family and not a trinity.

Certain people **are called according to the purpose that, whom He foreknew, He designates beforehand, also, to be conformed to the image of His Son, <u>for Him to be the Firstborn among many brethren</u> (Romans 8: 28-30).**

Jesus saved the world and is going to be the Firstborn of many brethren. This means that Jesus is creating people to be just like Him, His very brothers and sisters. This would not be possible if Jesus was part of a trinity. Christ Jesus did more than just save us from death; He was the first Son of God and is creating us to be sons and daughters of God as well. We are sons and daughters of God because and through Christ Jesus!

The spirit itself is testifying together with our spirit that we are children of God. Yet if children, enjoyers also of an allotment, enjoyers, indeed, of an allotment from God, yet joint enjoyers of Christ's allotment, if so be that we are suffering together, that we should be glorified together also (Romans 8: 16-17).

God gives belief to people that He designated beforehand to develop into the sons and daughters of God. These people are the first fruits of those that will enjoy the allotment of Jesus Christ. This is a special calling for selected human beings, but, if we continue reading in Romans 8 it is evident that all of creation is groaning for the revelation of the sons of God. Why does all creation want to know who the sons of God are? They also want to be freed from sin, corruption and death. **For to vanity was the creation subjected, not voluntarily, but because of Him Who subjects it, in expectation that the creation itself, also, shall be freed from the slavery of corruption into the glorious freedom of the <u>children of God</u>.**

Then, as scripture says, the rest of creation will put on the freedom of the children of God. You see, God is creating a family through Jesus Christ giving His creation the same attributes. Jesus was the first, and through Jesus, God will bring home all of His precious humans. Some He will bring into the family before others, but rest assured, God will one day be All in all. We will all be children of God because of Christ Jesus.

I would like to leave one final note on this topic. There are instances in scripture in which Jesus is praying to His Father, God. For example, Jesus prayed to God in the Garden of Gethsemane the night before His death. He also prayed on the cross. If Jesus and God are equal parts of the trinity, then was Jesus praying to Himself during these times? I don't think so. Now, Jesus does and did accomplish the will of God perfectly. He is the image of the invisible God, BUT, He is indeed the Son of God. Jesus **is the Image of the invisible God, firstborn of every creature (Colossians 1:15).** Jesus prayed in Gethsemane that there be another way to save the world besides crucifixion but He put God's will first. He prayed on the cross that God would forgive those in the process of killing Him. He did not run up to heaven to answer His own prayer. Jesus prayed to His Father, not Himself. Jesus died and did not exist for three days when He was in the grave. He was not alive in the form of the Father or in any other form or realm of existence. He was dead. Jesus was dead, asleep, just like we will one day be dead. Jesus was raised to new life and He will do the same for us at the resurrection...but not until the resurrection.

CHAPTER 4

GOD IS SOVEREIGN AND MAN DOES NOT HAVE A FREE-WILL

It was a balmy, ninety-two degrees as we took the thirty-eight minute drive to the tiny airport in northwest Indiana. My two young children were hearing the story of their great grandfather for the first time. A replica of the plane my grandfather co-piloted during World War II was awaiting us at the Porter Regional Airport. My grandfather passed away well before my children were born and he never really talked about his exploits during the war. But, I've heard the story many times and I tried to paraphrase as best I could to my son and daughter while I drove down the highway. The following excerpt is from a wonderful book that detailed the encounter.

Another round from the same burst did even more harm. Tondelayo's copilot, Lt. Edward J. Hicko, felt he wasn't doing anything productive while the pilot manhandled the damaged plane, so he pulled out his service automatic, cracked open the side window, wedged the gun barrel against the window frame, and popped away at Zeros. While he held the pistol in his right hand to reload it, a Japanese bullet pierced his back. The slug passed through his intestines, exited his lower abdomen, then nearly severed his right thumb before damaging the grip of the automatic. Due to the racket of gunfire and the engine outside his window, Hicko didn't realize immediately what had happened. The discovery of the wound stunned him; he refused to comprehend that he had been gut-shot.

The engineer, Staff Sgt. Weldon Ishler, was sickened by gas fumes. He punched a hole in the bulkhead of the bomb bay, discovered the damaged fuel line, and wrapped the line with a rag, using his bare hand as a clamp. This reduced the leak to a trickle, but he could not hold it indefinitely. Periodically, the radio operator took over. The fight rolled on. In the rear of Tondelayo, empty brass casings piled up beneath the turret. Up front, Hicko slumped in his seat, holding his hand against his abdomen as blood seeped between his fingers.

The enemy fighters would not slack off. Damage began to accrue. The turret gunner aboard SNAFU, Staff Sgt. Robert T. Henderson, was just as busy as Murphy. While frantically trying to reload his guns, Henderson was wounded by slugs that smashed through the Plexiglas. He fired a few more rounds before the guns were empty again. When the next enemy fighter bored in, he could only crouch behind the armor plate while bullets smacked all around him and chunks of Plexiglas rained down on his head.

Another crewmember aboard SNAFU, Staff Sgt. George M. Hardy Jr., was hit in the head. He made his way forward and got medical help from the navigator, Lt. Gerome A. Migliacci. While Migliacci administered first aid, a bullet sliced his ear and struck Hardy in the shoulder. Right after that, Migliacci noticed the fire. The bomb bay was crackling with bright flames, too involved already for a handheld fire extinguisher. But Migliacci tried anyway. Afterward, he moved forward and informed Anacker about the situation. The pilot merely glanced over his shoulder and nodded, then turned right, easing alongside the island's shoreline. If a fuel line had been hit, Anacker had to ditch quickly before a fuel tank blew.

- Excerpt from <u>Target: Rabaul: The Allied Siege of Japan's Most Infamous Stronghold, March 1943 – August 1945</u> by Bruce Gamble

The name of the aircraft was the Tondelayo and this was her most storied mission. They bombed several Japanese vessels and the crew fought valiantly in the sky of the South Pacific. I told this story as my children and I arrived at the airport to explore various World War II planes that were touring the country. We climbed aboard the Tondelayo and crawled throughout the plane trying to imagine what it was like for this noble crew during the war and especially on this specific mission. Then, my children took a seat in the co-pilot chair which was my grandfather's station. It sent chills up my spine to have my children share the co-pilot seat that was manned by my grandfather. But, as I snapped the picture and reminisced, another thought occurred to me.

My grandfather was shot in the back and the bullet pierced his intestines eleven times and then came out of his stomach and hit his thumb. Survival was slim, in fact, after the plane crashed a telegram was sent home to his wife informing her of his death. However, he did not die. Against all odds and a long recovery, my grandfather survived and lived for close to 50 healthy years after this event. Now, my children never met my grandfather but were enthralled with the story and loved crawling through the plane and sitting in the co-pilot's chair. It was an overall great experience.

Oftentimes I wonder what would have happened if my grandfather did not survive. My dad would have never been born and obviously never met my mom. I would not have been born. The ripple effect would have been tremendous. This leads me to think about when other people die or survive, the effect it has on future generations and their existence. How can all of this be so random in determining who will live and be born into this world. Well, the truth is that these decisions are made by God and they are not random at all. But instead, they are planned, ordained and orchestrated by God. He determines who will live and die and He determines who will be born. God is the placer of all things and all things have their being in His son, Jesus Christ.

Your eyes saw my embryo, And my days, all of them were written upon your scroll; The days, they were formed when there was not one of them (Psalm 139:16).

You see, God has planned out the details of each individual's life. He formed the days, what would happen in those days, when we would be born and when we will die. In fact, He formed each day and wrote it on his scroll to signify that it is set in stone. God planned each detail of our days before one of them came to be. In addition to this, God had this unalterable plan for us before we were even born, while He was forming us in the womb. *For You Yourself (God) achieved the making of my inmost being; You overshadowed me in my mother's belly (Psalm 139:13).*

My grandfather did fight for survival and he, I believe, was a very heroic man. However, his death was never in question. He was going to survive the gunshot wound and plane crash because God planned for it to happen that way. It might not have been a certainty from my grandfather's perspective, but from God's absolute prospective, my grandfather was going to live another fifty years.

I mentioned that one of the reasons I believe in the Holy Scriptures is because they point to a God who is in complete control of His creation. Just look at the order of life and the complexity of the human body. The handprint of intelligent design is on everything that our human eyes can see. However, the creation is tainted by evil which seems to throw God's plan off course. This is not the case, and later, we will discuss the purpose and plan for evil. Now, let's turn our attention to the scriptures that prove God is in control of His universe. Then, we will look at what He actually plans to do with us.

Ephesians chapter 1, verse 11 says: In Him we were also chosen, having been predestined according to the plan of Him <u>who works out everything in conformity with the purpose of His will.</u> With regard to our human choices that honor God, **for <u>it is God who works in you to will and to act according to His good purpose (Philippians 2:13).</u>** Everything means everything, your non-free will choices and all of your circumstances. The good things you do are done by God Who works in you to will and act according to His purpose. If God works out everything in conformity with the purpose of His will, then how can humans be free to do anything that is not in conformity with the purpose of His will? The answer is that they can't because free will is a myth. God conforms and dictates the good and evil in the world to work according to His predetermined and ultimate purpose.

Ephesians chapter 2, verses 8-10 goes on to say: For in grace, through faith, are you saved, and this is not of you; it is God's approach present, not of works lest anyone should be boasting. So, this is the way God is currently operating. This is how He was dealing with the people from Paul's time and the way He is dealing with the people of today. God is operating though grace and faith and He gives both of them to us. All the faith you have is from God for **God gives to each a measure of faith (Romans 12:3).** All the grace you have is from God. Humans are not responsible for any of this faith and grace, therefore we cannot boast. It is not up to us to make a choice for Jesus as some would say. That choice is made for us by God and was determined well before we were even born because God decided that He would give believers the faith to believe and the grace to be saved.

The rest of Ephesians chapter 2, verse 10 states: For His achievement are we, being created in Christ Jesus for good works, which God makes ready beforehand, that we should be walking in them. So we are being created in Jesus through God's own process. He is forming us as the scripture tells us we are His workmanship. It goes further, as being saved is a process of formation to become like Jesus, not a one-time event. We cannot do anything of ourselves or independently of God to be saved but God's grace will work in us to teach us, train us and give us what we need to be doing the very things God created us to do. Though we are doing and are actively involved in being created in Christ Jesus, it is all through the grace of God that is freely and one hundred percent given to us.

Next, the scripture that speaks of God making decisions before people are even outside the womb. Another testament to the sovereignty of God in the book of Romans recites the story of Jacob and Esau. It is God, not man that makes these choices.

Romans 9:13: Just as it is written: "Jacob I have loved, but Esau I hated." What then shall we say? Is God unjust? The writer asks the question as to whether God is unjust because God made the decision to have the older brother Esau serve the younger, Jacob. It was custom that the younger would serve the older. However, later in life Jacob tricked Esau out of his birth rite and got the blessing from his father Isaac. Jacob later became Israel.

So what! People are tricked out of things every day. Just look around and you have swindlers everywhere. So what's so special about Jacob and Esau? What's so special? God made all these decisions about the destiny of Jacob and Esau's lives before they were born, before they did anything good or bad. So, God had their entire destiny set. This was no little thing, as mentioned before, Jacob eventually was renamed Israel and we all know that the people of Israel play a major role in scripture. I conclude that if God would control the destiny of Jacob and Esau, then He controls the destiny of every human being.

Psalm 139:16 says: Your eyes saw my unformed body; all the days ordained for me were written in your book before one of them came to be. Before one day even happened, before the foundation of the world, God planned each day of our lives. These days are written, which means they cannot be changed or swayed in any way.

We started looking at **Romans 9:13-18** when we talked about Jacob and Esau now let's finish those verses. God says, **"I will have mercy on whom I have mercy, and I will have compassion on whom I have compassion." It does not, therefore, depend on man's effort, but on God's mercy.** For the scripture says to Pharaoh: **"I raised you up for** this very purpose, that I might display my power in you and that my name might be proclaimed in all the earth." Therefore <u>God has mercy on whom He wants to have mercy, and He hardens whom He wants to harden.</u>

Remember, Pharaoh was the one who kept God's people in captivity despite Moses continually pleading for their release. In these above mentioned verses, The Apostle Paul (Author of the book of Romans) says that man's effort is not the determining factor in how a man responds or acts towards God. He goes on to say that God has mercy on those He wants but also hardens those He wants. If God is responsible for hardening someone's heart, then it is not the person's free-will choice to reject God or act contrary to His plan. God planned it. Just like He did in the case of Pharaoh when he would not let God's people go. God did this for a reason, so that He might display His power and be proclaimed in all the earth. God has a reason for setting someone's heart against Him, we look more into the reasons God would do this in a later section. However, it is important to understand that it is God who directs the steps of man that lead to a hardened heart. **A man's steps are directed by the Lord. How then can anyone understand his own way (Proverbs 20:24)?**

Let's take a look at perhaps the most sobering scripture that shows that God's plan involves hardened hearts and evil bringing about his perfect will. **Acts 4:27-28: Indeed Herod and Pontius Pilate met together with the Gentiles and the people of Israel in this city to conspire against your holy servant Jesus, whom you anointed. <u>They did what Your power and will had decided beforehand should happen.</u>** Wow! Pilate, the man who allowed Jesus to be crucified by the high priest and Jewish allotment, did this because God's power and will decided that he should do this. This was planned beforehand, **since the creation of the world (Revelation 13:8).** Pilate chose to go along with crucifying God's own son because God put this in his heart. Pilate was just acting in accordance of God's predestined plan. As a result, Jesus's death and resurrection became a reality that will eventually save all people from death. God had to harden the hearts of Herod and Pilate in order to save the world through Jesus. It was not possible for Herod and Pilate to make any other decision. All works according to the plan of Almighty God. In fact, there is more to the above scripture. It was not just Herod and Pilate that conspired against Jesus.

The Gentiles and the people of Israel were also a part of supporting the torturing and death of Jesus. This was also decided beforehand by God. If God decided that all these people would act this way then these people were not free to act in any other way.

So, it is God that works in us to harden our hearts. Also, going back to **Philippians 2:13, it is God who works in you to will and to act according to His good purpose.** This proves that it is God working in us to produce our heart's intentions and actions of the flesh and spirit. Good or bad, in fact, **God has bound all men over to disobedience so that He may have mercy on them all (Romans 11:32).** God causes us to do good things and bad things, some more bad than good and vice versa. However, all of this is ordained by God, going back to **Ephesians 1:11, Who works out everything in conformity with the purpose of His will.**

Now, I am not saying that man does not make choices. We make choices every day and we will be held accountable for these choices. However, these choices are a product of a human nature and circumstances of life. God is in control of every circumstance and shapes every human to act according to their circumstances and nature in order to carry out a destiny in which the Lord has already set.

Does the ax raise itself above him who swings it, or the saw boast against him who uses it? As if a rod were to wield him who lifts it up, or a club brandish him who is not wood! This verse in Isaiah 10:15 is speaking to the fact that we are controlled by the Almighty God. We cannot walk outside of His predetermined will for us. We have as much free will as an ax does when a person swings it. The ax is under complete control. We are the ax is God's hands...or perhaps a better illustration is that we are clay in God's hands. In the book of Romans, this exact comparison is made, that God is the potter and we are the clay. **Does not the potter have the right to make out of the same lump of clay some pottery for special purposes and some for common use (Romans 9:21)?** How can anyone believe the scriptures and believe that we have a free will at the same time? You have to ignore half of the bible and discard scripture after scripture in order to deny the sovereignty of God. Humans want to have a free will but scripture plainly says that man has no free will. Therefore, you will be left with the choice of believing what man wants to believe or believing what the bible actually says.

In Isaiah 14:24, God actually states in the first person, **"Surely, as I have planned, so it will be, and as I have purposed, so it will stand."** This does not sound like a God who allows His plans to be thwarted by humans, Satan or any other power in the universe. We will get to Satan's purpose and the role of evil. Rest assured though, they are part of God's plan not an exception to it. If that's not enough, then **Isaiah 46: 10-11** certainly states the certainty of God's plan. Isaiah is quoting God here:

I make known the end from the beginning, from ancient times, what is still to come. I say, "My purpose will stand, and I will do all that I please." From the east I summon a bird of prey; from a far-off land, a man to fulfill my purpose. What I have said, that I will bring about; what I have planned, that I will do.

It is perhaps the most difficult truth to come to terms with, especially for us Americans who were taught that no one can tell us what to do. The truth that we are not the masters of our fate, that we are not the captain of our soul. To believe that God is directing our steps and has predetermined each and every detail of our lives before we were even born is difficult because we want to be in control, at least a little. You want to start an argument a party, tell someone they don't have free will and see what happens. Now, I am not saying that people do not have a will, because they do. However, if they have "Free-will" then this would need to be free from any outside influence. However, every choice we make is caused by some circumstance. Some would object, "I can choose to be a fan of any NFL football team, but I use my free-will to root for the Chicago Bears." Well, yes, that is your choice. But, it is not free. So many things are working to cause you to be a Bears fan. Perhaps you live in Chicago, you have preference towards certain players, you like the uniforms, you like sports, you like football. However, if you grew up in Green Bay or didn't like sports, your preference would be different.

Anyway, perhaps a poor example, but, the bottom line is that scripture states that God works in humans and creates circumstances that cause people to act according to his plan and foreknowledge. Well, what about sin? Surely, if someone sins, God did not plan or have anything to do with them sinning.

Have you ever heard the story of Abimelek?

Abraham moved to a new region and told the leader of this region that Sarah was his sister, when in fact, she was his wife. Abraham was worried that once the people in this area saw Sarah's beauty, they would kill him and take Sarah. Abimelek, upon seeing Sarah, took her. God informed Abimelek in a dream that indeed Sarah was a married woman. Abimelek protested that even though he was tricked by Abraham and Sarah, he did not touch Sarah. **Then God said to him in the dream, "Yes, I know you did this with a clear conscience, and so I have kept you from sinning against me. That is why I did not let you touch her (Genesis 20:6).**

Here we have a plain statement from God that He actually kept someone from sin and did not let a person do a sinful action. This is God's work, not the supposed free-will of man. If God can stop one man from sinning, then couldn't He stop all men from sinning? A sovereign God certainly could. However, as we will see soon, sin plays a major role and has an intended purpose within God's divine plan. All is of God and nothing can operate outside of His intended purpose.

Okay, I am going to take a break before we get into God's sovereign act of calling the Apostle Paul. We have discussed that God is in control and that control cannot be altered by man in any way. Men, women and children cannot surprise God by their actions. Indeed, God's foreknowledge makes it impossible for free will to be true. Think about this: If God knows what we will do in the future, then we are not free to make any other choice than what God knows is going to happen. However, scripture says that God's sovereignty and foreknowledge goes much deeper that just knowing what is going to happen. We have already discussed many of these scriptures. However, another scripture that hits on this point is **Isaiah 46:10** where God says **I make known the end from the beginning, from ancient times, what is still to come. "I say, My purpose will stand, and I will do all that I please."**

In the above mentioned scripture, God knows the end, how things will turn out. He has the end in mind and the exact outcome from the very beginning. He declares what has happened in the past and what will happen in the future. Nothing can change this as God says His purpose will stand and He will do all that He Pleases. So no human is free to act in a way that is separate to what God has declared. Therefore, no man has a 'Free-will.' The future is as set in stone as the past and humans cannot act contrary to God's will for the future as much as they cannot go back and change the past.

So if God is sovereign and runs His creation exactly the way He wants, what is His purpose and desire? I believe this is stated in **1 Timothy 2:4: For this is ideal and welcome in the sight of our Savior, God, Who wills that all mankind be saved and come into a realization of the truth.** Does God really will that all men be saved? If He is a God of love, He certainly would. Also, is this just a weak, unattainable wish of God that will not come true? Does God desire to save all men but cannot because of the free-will of man? Well, the words of scripture answer these questions and crush the notion that God cannot get exactly what He wants. Man cannot stop the will of God. God wills all men to be saved and every last one of them will be saved. God wills every man, woman and child to be saved and **He works out everything in conformity with the purpose of His will (Ephesians 1:11). For it is God who works in you to will and to act according to His good purpose (Philippians 2:13). A man's steps are directed by the Lord (Proverbs 20:24).** God says, **"Surely, as I have planned, so it will be, and as I have purposed, so it will stand (Isaiah 14:24)."**

Now, I am sure there are objectors that would argue God does not force us to do things and that humans make choices all the time. Well, we do make choices and we certainly have an illusion of freedom in those choices. However, every scripture in the bible will attest that we cannot act independently from God. The almighty has ordained the end from the beginning and has planned every detail of our lives. The circumstances of our life, how we react, and the way God created us will lead us into the very decisions that God has planned for us to make. Just like when **Isaiah 10:15 asks: Does the axe raise itself above the one who swings it, or the saw boast against the one who uses it?** In the same sense, man cannot act separate from God and do his own thing. That is how absurd the notion of free-will is when it comes to the scriptures. God says that believing in free will is the same as believing that the axe and the saw act independently of the person using them. The next time you use or see someone using an axe or a saw, just observe and see if those tools can do whatever they want or if they are under complete control. If you believe that the axe and saw do their own thing than that is as ridiculous as believing that man has free-will. Sorry if this is a difficult pill to swallow but scripture after scripture prove this point. If anyone believes in free-will, they must ignore countless verses and stories in the bible that prove God is sovereign and that man is clay in His hands.

We, as humans cannot do good on our own. We need God operating in us to give us the faith, grace and love that we need to act according to His delight. This is illustrated again in **Jeremiah 13:23** when the following question is posed**: Can an Ethiopian change his skin or a leopard its spots? Neither can you do good who are accustomed to doing evil.** It is impossible for a leopard to change his spots and for a man to change his skin color. God equates this to how it is impossible for man to act good without the divine influence of God. We need God's influence, which is His grace, in order to do the good things of God and to bring us out of evil. This is not free-will; it is God's gracious action upon us.

One more story for you. A story about a man named Saul of Tarsus. This is an important story because this man held the coats of men who stoned Stephen, a servant of Jesus Christ. Saul approved of killing this believer and many more. However, this man became the greatest missionary in the history of the world, the apostle Paul. He wrote thirteen letters in the New Testament! Paul writes this about himself and the grace he received: **But for that very reason I was shown mercy so that in me, the worst of sinners, Christ Jesus might display his unlimited patience as an example for those who would believe on him and receive eternal life (1 Timothy 1:16).**

You see, Paul was once Saul, his name was changed at his conversion. Saul was on his way to persecute and arrest believers in Jesus Christ. This man broke into houses in the middle of the night with his goons and dragged men, women and children out of their homes. He opposed Christ more than anyone as he proclaimed to be the worst of sinners. He had no intention of repenting, choosing to believe, accepting Christ, or even seeking any other truth. Saul hated Christ and his followers! Yet, in a moment, chapter 9 of the book of Acts tells us that he was knocked off his horse and the Lord Jesus Christ himself told him, "**Now get up and go into the city, and you will be told what you must do.**" Jesus did not give him a free will choice, nor could Saul's decision be free after such a terrific circumstance of being blinded by the risen Christ. The Lord later appeared to a disciple named Ananias and said regarding Saul, "**Go! This man is my chosen instrument to carry my name before the gentiles and the kings and before the people of Israel (Acts 9:15).**

The Lord changed Saul's name to Paul and he became the single greatest missionary in history. Paul spread the good news of Jesus Christ in his time. However, as mentioned before, his letters to the early believers make up a big portion of the New Testament of the bible. So, how many more throughout history are being saved by reading the New Testament and Paul's words. Do you really think God left the vessel that would be such a significant part of his plan, to chance? Or worse yet, left it to the mercy of Saul's free will choice? No. The bible says that Paul was chosen since the beginning of time (2 Timothy 1: 9-10). Paul was chosen by God before he took one step toward Jesus Christ! He was on his way to kill and torture Christians. He did not choose Jesus Christ to be saved, Jesus Christ chose him. Remember, the apostle Paul says that his conversion will be an example for those who believe and receive eternal life. Now, we all probably will not see the Risen Lord in this life, but what the apostle is getting at is the example of Jesus choosing us and giving us transcending grace, through nothing we have done.

This leads to probably, in my view, the most decisive scripture that proves man does not make a free-will choice to come to Jesus. It is **2 Timothy 1:9-10: who has saved us and called us to a holy life–<u>not because of anything we have done but because of his own purpose and grace. This grace was given us in Christ Jesus before the beginning of time</u>, but it has now been revealed through the appearing of our Savior, Christ Jesus, who has destroyed death and has brought life and immortality to light through the gospel.**

Christian preachers will tell you that "You" and "You" alone need to make a decision to accept Jesus Christ. This is an action or a "doing something" on our parts. However, the above mentioned scripture tells us that we are saved based on nothing we have done. We are saved because God chose to save us and this decision was made before the beginning of time. How can we possibly believe that we made a free-will decision to be saved? We just can't, if we believe these scriptures. Believers were chosen before they were even born, before sin was even a problem. How are they free to be anything other than what God called them to be.

God knows humanity because He created our inmost being and knit us together in our mother's womb (Psalm 139:13). He chose when and where we would be born and put specific people around us while orchestrating all circumstances to bring about His plan within us. God chooses to save some people now and He chooses to save the rest later. This is done by God's design and in His timing. Nothing we can do will change that. Nothing, absolutely nothing, is free to operate outside of God's intended purpose.

I understand that coming to the realization that we do not have free-will is one of the most difficult truths to comprehend. We want to be in control of our lives. However, that is why the belief in free-will is one of Satan's greatest weapons to put our faith in us and not God. If you don't believe me, tell the next person you see that free-will does not exist and see what happens. Sorry, that is what the scriptures clearly teach. You can believe these plain statements or not. I think it is comforting to know that I cannot screw up my destiny and that my destiny is held by a God filled with love and one who has a far better plan for me than I could even imagine. We clearly make thousands of choices each day and it appears that we make those choices of our own volition. But, none of those choices are free from the influence of God. He directs us even when we have the perception of making our own way.

As far as religion goes, free will is taught because, especially in Christianity, they need a scapegoat. They need to blame eternal hell on the person to get God of the hook. None of the choices we make are without influence so they are not free. God is in control of our circumstances and indeed He holds our entire being.

Grace and self-will

Grace is one of the most difficult things in the world to comprehend. I think this is because we are taught from a very young age that if you do what is right good things will happen and if you do what is wrong bad things will happen. We are disciplined by parents, teachers and other authority figures using reward and punishment based on our actions. This system has its place for sure but must be abandoned to truly embrace the death and resurrection of Jesus Christ. Grace is completely unmerited and you can do nothing to earn it. The moment a person does a good work or refrains from doing an evil deed to earn grace, then grace is no longer grace as you did or did not do something to earn it. Grace is the absolute, finished work of Jesus Christ given to us. Yes, we may need to do specific works or become something, be trained. But, this is all of God from start to finish.

Every religion in the world, including Christianity has at least some to-do list in order to earn salvation from a deity. Muslims, Hindus, Buddhists, Jews and every denomination of Christianity teach that a person must do certain things or they will go to an eternal hell. Those are the major religions but you can add any sect or any other religion and you will come up with the same result, even if at first, like Christianity, it appears that they rely on faith and not works.

Most Christians will say that you are saved by Jesus Christ through faith. However, they don't realize that that faith is a gift from God. They say that you need to make a free will choice to believe in Jesus to activate His death and resurrection. No sir! No Mam! Either Jesus died for us or He didn't. Our belief does not change what He did nor does our choice activate anything. Christians will tell you that it is your belief in Jesus that will save; His actual death and resurrection saved no one. Not true, Jesus was tortured for hours on the cross and then died. The Almighty Son of God secured your destiny, along with everyone's destiny. It is a done deal; Jesus saved you no matter what. Belief will come in God's timing for each individual person. Those who come into the realization of God's truth will enter sooner, the others will enter later.

With that being said, I want to clarify that I am no expert on grace. I do not believe people will be saved in continuing in sinful ways. Yes, they will be saved but not by continuing in their sin. They will be corrected by grace and will go through a difficult process of being saved. Jesus has saved all by His death and resurrection but many people will turn from their sinful ways before they come home. Again, the whole process is of God.

God has created each and every one of us uniquely and has a unique plan, an individual plan, to bring each of us home. Our hearts, no matter how hard now, will one day be throbbing with joy. We will have the greatest possible joy, peace, love, happiness and all good things once God has completed us.

CHAPTER 5

GOD CREATED EVIL FOR A PURPOSE

It is popular belief that Lucifer, a mighty archangel, rebelled against God and was cast out of heaven. Therefore, starting the process of evil and ruining God's perfect creation and ever since, wreaking havoc on humanity. I am not going to dissect the lack of support for this theory in scripture. There are a few verses that are taken out of context from which this belief has grown. However, I am going to focus on the words of God when it comes to evil.

God said, **"I form the light and create darkness, I bring prosperity and <u>create evil;</u> I, the Lord, do all these things (Isaiah 45:7). It is from the mouth of the Most High that both evil and good things come (Lamentations 3:38).** One more in **Amos 3:6: Would there come to be evil in a city and Yahweh not have done it?** Here we have God speaking in the first person and another blatant statement in scripture that God is the author of evil. The word used in these scriptures is the Hebrew word "Ra" and it means evil. It is the same word used to describe the people of Noah's day that were wiped off the face of the earth. There can be no doubt that God created this evil if you read these scriptures. Okay then, why would an almighty, sovereign, loving God create evil?

Let's go back to the garden for a moment. God planted a tree in the middle of the garden of which Adam and Eve were instructed not to eat. This tree was the "Tree of the Knowledge of Good and Evil." This tree was part of God's creation that He deemed, very good! How can a tree that has evil be deemed, very good? Not only that, but this tree was put in the middle of the garden and was pleasing to the eye. Why didn't God make an evil tree and a good tree and then instruct Adam and Eve to eat from the good tree and not the evil tree? The answer is because evil and good are so related to one another that they had to share the same tree. In essence, you cannot fully know good if you do not have an experience of evil. Evil is used to create us into the glorious beings we will one day be.

Mark 7:21 and Matthew 15:19 say that it is <u>out of the heart</u> that evil thoughts come. Now, here is the bible's account of Eve: **When the woman saw that the fruit of the tree was good for food and pleasing to the eye, and also desirable for gaining wisdom, she took some and**

ate it. She also gave some to her husband, who was with her, and he ate it (Genesis 3:6). Adam and Eve desired this fruit before they ate it, remember, it is out of the heart that evil thoughts come. I believe that Adam's heart and Eve's heart contained the evil thoughts of disobeying God and eating the fruit. Yes, the serpent encouraged this and may have even planted the seed, but it was still the hearts' of Adam and Eve that desired the fruit and its benefits. This was evil. So, what is my point?

My point is, and this destroys most of Christian Doctrine, that Adam and Eve were not created perfect and God intended them to eat of the forbidden tree. Yes, God instructed them not to eat of this tree, but **God has bound everyone over to disobedience so that He may have mercy on them all (Romans 11:32).** I believe that mankind was created to disobey God and sin.

Why would something this horrific be a part of God's plan? Well, God is creating us to become like His son, Jesus Christ, having all of his attributes. However, in order to fully understand the goodness of God, we need to go through an experience of evil. It is the contrast principle. We need to know evil in order to fully understand what good is and just how good God is. Adam and Eve did not know evil so they didn't have much of a clue what good was or how good they had it. God's creation is perfect, and evil is a part of creating us, perfect.

I do not understand how God "Created us in His image" and then we did something that He would never do...we sinned! Being created in the image of someone else means that you are almost identical. Think of it, when someone says, "You have the image of your father." But, we as humans are the complete opposite of what God is. Adam and Eve sinned which means they are nowhere and were never anywhere in the ballpark of being in God's image. This only makes sense once we understand that God's plan is not done. He is not finished creating us. Evil, sin and death will be passed through for each human before they are perfected. Then, once we are truly sons of God and evil and death have served their purpose, they will be done away with and destroyed forever. Then, we will be perfected sons and daughters that have the image of our Father.

As we will see soon, Jesus took our sin and experienced evil and death. He didn't just die for us; He showed us the way to become like Him. Jesus showed us that we must go through evil and death, just like He did in order to get to our resurrected, perfected state. We still experience evil and death despite believing in Jesus Christ, so He did not save us from these things. Instead, He saved us through these things. They are part of the process. Then, when we become like Jesus; sin, evil and death are no more.

For our struggle is not against flesh and blood, but <u>against the rulers, against the authorities, against the powers of this dark world and against the spiritual forces of evil in the heavenly realms</u> (Ephesians 6:12). Our battle of sin and death are against the rulers, authorities, and powers of this dark world, against the spiritual forces of evil in the heavenly realms. I have underlined certain words because they are the same words used in the next set of scripture that prove that God created these powers and forces.

He is the image of the invisible God, the firstborn over all creation. <u>For by him all things were created: things in heaven and on earth, visible and invisible, whether thrones or powers or rulers or authorities; all things were created by him and for him.</u> He is before all things, and in him all things hold together. And he is the head of the body, the church; he is the beginning and the firstborn from among the dead, so that in everything he might have the supremacy. For God was pleased to have all his fullness dwell in him, and through him to reconcile to himself all things, whether things on earth or things in heaven, by making peace through his blood, shed on the cross (Colossians 1: 15-20).

All things, including evil entities were created by God and for God, and He will reconcile all these things to Himself by the blood of Jesus shed on the cross. Evil, all people, all creation, all things will be reconciled to God.

Satan and Fire

Let's take a brief look at part of the purpose of fire (flames) and Satan as presented in scripture. In 1 Corinthians 3:15, Paul is talking about a person's life work. He writes, **if it is burned up, he will suffer loss; he himself will be saved, but only as one escaping through the flames.** The flames act as a purification tool to destroy everything that is bad so that a person will be saved. Can it be that all mention of flames in the bible has a purifying effect on a person rather than just being used for torturing people in hell? The bible says that Jesus baptizes with the Holy Spirit and fire. That fire is a divine fire that produces good. Perhaps the lake of fire mentioned in Revelations has an extreme purifying effect on all who enter. Therefore, this fire may be purging away everything that kept people from believing in Christ until they finally escape through the flames with the truth.

How about the role of Satan? **When you are assembled in the name of our Lord Jesus and I am with you in spirit, and the power of our Lord Jesus is present, hand this man over to Satan, so that the sinful nature may be destroyed and his spirit saved on the day of the Lord (1 Corinthians 5: 4-5).** In this verse, Paul was talking about a man who had committed horrible sins in the church, such as, having sex with his father's wife. Think about that. Surely this man would be cast into hell to burn for all eternity. Hand him over to Satan to be tortured! Wait. This man was handed over to Satan, but, not to be tortured in hell. This horribly sinful man was handed over to Satan so that his sinful nature will be destroyed so that his spirit can be saved. What? Are you saying that Satan plays a role in salvation? No, I am not, scripture is. Satan wreaks havoc and evil on all of creation, but is ultimately under the control of God.

All is from God, all has its existence through God, and all will come back to God in its own time. Evil and Satan are a part of what God uses to bring about salvation and the greatest possible everlasting good for each and every human being. Christians say that unbelievers will be cast into the lake of fire, which the bible says is the second death. They say that unbelievers will stay in this state forever. However, the bible says that all death will be destroyed. What happens to the unbelievers in the lake of fire when death is completely destroyed or rendered inoperative? The answer is that they will be purified and come to accept Christ. Therefore, at a later time, these unbelievers will become believers and will be redeemed.

For his anger lasts only a moment, but his favor lasts a lifetime; weeping may remain for a night, but rejoicing comes in the morning (Psalm 30:5).

I heard a song on the radio a few days ago in which the singer was bashing his ex-girlfriend or something like that. It said that she raised him up only to bring him down. It was a horrible song, but I thought that this is God, if you turn the words completely around.

God brings us down to raise us up. God brings us down through sin, evil and death so that Jesus can raise us up. We will be stronger and reach our full, unimaginable Joy, peace, love and happiness because we went through this process. Our hearts will one day be throbbing with joy, but first, Just like Jesus on the cross, we need to feel forsaken by God. In the end, feeling alienated from God for a period of time will bring us closer to Him. Though we are never outside His will, it certainly feels as though we are. However, God is working through this to create us into His own son and daughter to enjoy everlasting life with Him.

CHAPTER 6

IS GOD TRULY ALL-LOVING AND ALL-POWERFUL?

So we have looked at scripture that shows that God is sovereign and uses evil to accomplish his mission. Now, let's look at what God wants to accomplish or what His will actually is: **God wants (wills) all men to be saved and to come to the knowledge of the truth (1 Timothy 2:4).** This is God's will and it is His intention to accomplish. This is why understanding that man does not have free will and that God is sovereign is so important. If we believe that we can act independently from God, then we make **1 Timothy 2:4** a weak wish from a pathetic god.

It comes down to whether we actually believe that God is all-loving and all-powerful. Sure, Christians and other factions will say that He is, but do they actually believe it? If God wants all men to be saved but cannot save them, or they end up in some eternal hell, can God really be all-powerful? He cannot even bring His own creation into submission of His own desires. Therefore, the belief is that human free-will (if someone chooses to reject Christ in this life) is stronger than the will of God. So, in essence, God cannot achieve His will and is at the mercy of man's free-will. This belief flies in the face of all the scripture that point to God's sovereign power. On the other hand, some will argue that God does not will or want every human being to be saved, thus retaining His all-powerful status. But, He has predestined some people to be created only for their end to be eternal torture in hell or annihilation. In that case, God created humans for the sole purpose of torturing them and doesn't even want to save them. Therefore, God could not possibly be all loving.

The only way God can be all loving and all powerful is if He loves enough to will all people to be saved and then has the power to complete His will. The Holy Scriptures attest to the fact that God will do this very thing. It is religion that denies the truth of God and then attaches the name of Jesus to their lies.

If you believe scripture, I don't think one can debate the fact that God chooses and predestines. **For those God foreknew He also predestined to be conformed to the image of His son…(Romans 8:29). So God does as He pleases with the powers of heaven and <u>the peoples of earth</u>. No one can hold back his hand or say to him: What have you done (Daniel**

4:35). God can do what He wants and the bible says that He **wants all men to be saved (1 Timothy 2:4).** Free will, nor any power in the universe, whether real or imagined, can hold back His hand.

Some people, especially Christians, will argue: God did not make us robots! No, He didn't make us robots. But, we are clay in His hands; the bible is clear on that. This argument that "God did not make us robots and wants us to love Him because we choose to love Him" doesn't make any sense when you look at it. Why doesn't this make any sense? It doesn't make any sense because it assumes that we are free from all sources of influence. The scriptures are riddled with verses that prove that humans are influenced by the flesh, Satan and many other forces. Therefore, if God stepped aside and required us to choose Him on our own, it still would not be free. We would still be influenced by our carnality and circumstances. That is why **"No one can come to me unless the Father who sent me draws them, and I will raise them up on the last day (John 6:44)."** Jesus' own words, repeatedly, tell us that God brings people to His son. Otherwise, we would all remain blinded. **The god of this age** (Satan) **has blinded the eyes of unbelievers, so that they cannot see the light of the gospel that displays the glory of Christ, who is the image of God (2 Corinthians 4:4).** We cannot come to God until God chooses to bring us to Him. It is by His will, His love and His timing.

Now, I believe the scriptures are clear that God, through Jesus Christ will save every single person who did, is and will walk the face of the earth, but that does not mean there is no process to salvation. Before I get into the process, clarification may be needed. I do not believe that anyone will be saved apart from Jesus Christ. Unitarian Universalism and other religions believe that nothing matters and people just go to some paradise when they die. They don't put any stock into what a person believes. I simply do not believe this and it is scripturally inaccurate. The truth is that I do believe all humanity will be with God, however, they will have everlasting life with God because of the life, death and resurrection of Jesus Christ. Everyone will be saved, but each one will be saved by Jesus Christ, individually. There is no other way to be saved. **Salvation is found in no one else, for there is no other name under heaven given to mankind by which we must be saved (Acts 4:12). Jesus answered, "I am the way the truth and the life. No one comes to the Father except through me (John 14:6)."**

CHAPTER 7

Is Jesus a Failure or Did He Do His Job on Earth?

Jesus Christ had a stated mission to accomplish while he was on earth. **The Son of God appeared to destroy the devil's work (1 John 3:8), to seek and to save that which was lost (Luke 19:10) and to save sinners (1 Timothy 1:15).** Now, Jesus says that he has accomplished this will according to his own words. **"I have brought you** (God) **glory on earth by completing the work you gave me to do (John 17:4).** The scripture says that Jesus completed the work of destroying the devil's work which is sin and death, seeking and saving the lost and saving sinners. Therefore, if one sinner remains or one person is lost forever, this verse would not be true. However, **John 17:4** is true because through Jesus, every man woman and child will be saved. Every lost sinner that is the victim of the devil's work will one day be with God.

Why again did Jesus appear? **He appeared once for all at the end of the ages to do away with sin by the sacrifice of himself (Hebrews 9:26).** I need to repeat that, "Jesus appeared to do away with sin." The bible says that He accomplished His mission. Yes, sin is still prevalent in the world, which is obvious if one just looks around. So is death. However, Jesus' death and resurrection made certain that sin and death will one day be destroyed and at God's desired time, all of this will come to pass. Sin and death will become inoperative. They will not be operating in a corner of the universe or in some alternate dimension called eternal hell. Sin and death will not keep people dead as annihilationist' teach. Sin and death will be gone and all that will be left is life. Everlasting life and immortality for every human being that has ever lived.

I will get back to the scriptures that prove that sin and death will be destroyed and all will be with God, in a moment. For now, let's focus on Jesus Christ and what He actually was and is, the savior of the world.

Savior versus potential savior

The bible says that Jesus is the savior of the world. However, most people believe that Jesus is the potential savior of the world. How can this be? Surely Jesus cannot be the savior of those whom he does not save. But scripture indicates that He is the savior of the whole world, not just believers of the world or part of the world, but the whole world. Why is the word **WHOLE** used in the bible?

My point is that others and Jesus Himself cannot claim to be the savior of the world unless He actually saves the world. Otherwise, He should be referred to as "The savior of all who believe," or "The savior of those who do right," or "The savior of those who have faith," or "The savior of those that chose Him." If one person ends up dead or separated from God for all eternity, then Jesus is not that person's savior because that person is not saved. Jesus was not called the potential savior of the world; He was called and is "The Savior of the World."

The next day John saw Jesus coming toward him and said, "Look, the Lamb of God, who takes away the sin of the world."
   -   John 1:29

Notice that John did not say, "Look, the Lamb of God, who takes away the sin of believers, or those who will follow him." John the Baptist said that Jesus takes away the sin of the world, not part of the world. The bible makes it clear that it is important to believe that Jesus is our savior and to become believers. Scripture does indeed say that we are saved by grace through faith in Jesus Christ. However, what scripture does not say, is that God's saving power or Jesus' ability to take away sin is limited to whether one is a believer in this life.

"And He himself (Jesus Christ) is the propitiation for our sins (believers), and not for ours only but also for the <u>whole world</u>."
   -   1 John 2:2

This scripture is written from the point of view of a community of believers. These believers say that Jesus Christ died for their sins, which is rightly so. However, they also say that Christ did not die for their sins only. This letter says that Jesus died for the **Whole World.** Yes, the believers have a special salvation and knowledge of the fact that Jesus Christ is the atonement for their sins. But, this atonement is also for the whole world.

Not potential atonement for the whole world, but actual atonement for the whole world.

That is, that God was in Christ reconciling the world to Himself, not imputing their trespasses to them, and has committed to us the world of reconciliation.
- **2 Corinthians 5:19**

This verse in 2ⁿᵈ Corinthians tells us that Christ is reconciling the world to himself! It is not segmenting or excluding anything. This verse simply says that God, in Christ, is going to reconcile the world. If Christ is not reconciling the whole world, then why wouldn't this scripture say that God was in Christ reconciling those who believe to Himself. Simply, it does not say that, it says the world. And as we will discover later, some are saved in this life and the rest will be saved later. This constitutes the world that this particular scripture is referencing.

"For to this end we both labor and suffer reproach, because we trust in the living God, who is the savior of all men, especially of those who believe."
- **1 Timothy 4:10**

This is the scripture that began to open my eyes to the fact that Jesus Christ would save all of humanity. This verse says that God is the savior of all men. How could He be the savior of all men if He did not save all men? But, not even that, the next word is the clincher. Paul says that God is the savior of all men, <u>especially</u> those who believe. Notice he does not say God is the savior of only or exclusively those who believe, but especially. The "especially" qualifies the rest of the group as being saved or God being their savior and remember, God cannot be their savior if He does not actually save them. This means that believers have a special salvation, but unbelievers will have salvation and eventually come to God through Jesus Christ.

Philippians chapter 2: 10-11 states, "That at the name of Jesus every knee shall bow, of those in heaven, and of those on earth, and of those under the earth, and that every tongue shall confess that Jesus

Christ is Lord, to the glory of God the Father." This clearly means all people, right? Yes, it does. It includes people on the earth, in heaven and under the earth. That means everybody. Every person, according to these verses, is confessing that Jesus Christ is Lord.

Scripture says that only the spirit can confess Jesus as Lord, and here, all humanity is making the confession unto salvation. Now, some may say that this is a forced confession. They may say that even unbelievers will be forced to confess Jesus as Lord even when they are in hell. However, verse 11 says that this confession of Jesus Christ is to the glory of God the Father. Would it really glorify the father if this was a forced confession? If these people actually rejected God's loving gift of his Son and therefore God failed to redeem them through His Son and therefore these people will spend an eternity in a pit of flames, how would that bring God any glory? The answer is that it wouldn't. This thought might make Christians happy and self-righteous, but certainly not the loving God.

These confessions do bring God glory, however. They bring Him glory because these confessions are heartfelt from transformed human beings that have been saved. Remember, **Philippians, chapter 2: 10-11** clearly talks about all people. What would bring God more glory? God Being able to save a fraction of humanity or being able to save all humanity through the work of his son? All humanity! This is what these verses speak of: The glory of God saving all of humanity, and every last person confessing this to His glory. This is a humanity that has overcome sin and death through Jesus Christ. This is the truth of scripture!

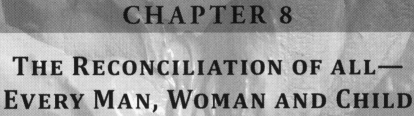

CHAPTER 8

THE RECONCILIATION OF ALL—
EVERY MAN, WOMAN AND CHILD

On a hot, humid summer night, the family of four slept quietly in their home. It was as any other night until the spark ravaged throughout the house destroying everything in its path. The kitchen wiring was faulty and this is where the fire began. The flames moved through each room one at a time. Now, it was surrounding and beginning to invade the very bedrooms of mom and dad and the two children that lay sleeping. The smoke was so thick now that nothing could be seen and most would stay asleep. Only mom awoke to be disoriented and overcome with the smoke. She soon returned to her unconscious state and all were helpless and approaching certain death as smoke filled their lungs as they lay passed out.

Mr. Shumway was nothing much to please the eyes. He was short with a medium build with more hair on his face than on his head. That night, he noticed the flames pouring out the windows from his house across the street. Mr. Shumway knew the family across the street well. He loved children and he would always try to teach his neighbors something new every day. On this night, Mr. Shumway did not hesitate. He ran across the street and entered the burning house as time was short. He dodged flames and covered his nose and mouth as he ran through the hallway and turned to go up the stairs as he knew the bedrooms were there. Going to his knees to dodge flames and inhale less smoke, he crawled into the children's room and scooped them up, one in each arm. Somehow, he could not even recall later, Mr. Shumway was able to maneuver around the flames and get the kids outside away from the fire.

The heroic neighbor was not done, he entered the house two more times to go into the bedroom on the other side of the upstairs hallway to first carry mom and then dad out of the house. By this time, some neighbors crowded the streets outside and an ambulance and fire truck arrived. The family of four woke up hours later, each in their own hospitable bed oblivious to what had happened. They all survived and would make full recoveries. However, Mr. Shumway received serious burns and was overcome by smoke as he collapsed outside the burning house after the last victim was saved. He died in the hospitable bed next to the rooms of the people that were saved.

As the family of four reunited and recovered, some of the other neighbors that gathered around the home came to the hospital to explain what had happened. The family had no recollection of the nights' events. Neighbor one came to the family and explained the heroics of Mr. Shumway. He explained how Shumway ran into the house and pulled them out of the fire. However, neighbor one continued to speak about how the family must get up, exercise, eat well and follow specific rules in order to be saved from the fire. Neighbor one then left the room and as the family was thinking about this message, neighbor two walked through the door.

Neighbor two entered the room to speak though she was still in her own house when the fire and rescue took place earlier that night. She had heard from other neighbors what had happened and felt she needed to relay this information to the family. Neighbor two explained the actions of Mr. Shumway and what he did for them. Then, neighbor two explained that the family would need to believe in Mr. Shumway and what he did in order to be saved from the flames of the fire. The family was now even more confused than they were after neighbor one left. So too, neighbor two left the hospital room.

In came neighbor three, he was on the other side of town when the fire occurred. He drove straight to the hospital after he had heard about the fire. Neighbor three did not like Mr. Shumway very much as they did not see eye to eye on many issues. As a result, neighbor three refused to believe that Mr. Shumway saved the family. He explained with anger and hatred that Shumway was not a good man and could not do anything to help when the fire ravaged through the house. Now the family was dumbfounded and really did not know what to believe. Neighbor three stomped out of the room elated about how he dragged Mr. Shumway's name through the mud.

Neighbor four entered and explained the story in detail about what happened to the family that evening. He was an even-tempered, calm, peaceful man. Neighbor four's demeanor was different from the previous three neighbors. It seemed that he was not there to accomplish anything or complete an agenda. He simple explained what Mr. Shumway had done for the family. He explained how he fought the flames and brought their four, unconscious bodies out of the flames and sacrificed his own life to save theirs. Neighbor four explained to the family that they are saved because of Mr. Shumway. The family understood neighbor four and went and lived their lives continually in a state of thanksgiving for Mr. Shumway. However, even when they faltered, they know that Mr. Shumway had saved them and nothing could ever change that.

The above story is about a man who sacrificed his own life to save others and is used to illustrate what Jesus Christ did for us. After Mr. Shumway gave his life for the family, two neighbors approached and told the family what they must now do to be saved. Neighbor one explained that they needed to do certain things or follow some rules. Neighbor two said the family had to believe in what Mr. Shumway had done for them in order to be saved. The third neighbor didn't believe that Mr. Shumway saved them at all. However, it does not matter if the family followed any of these three neighbors' stories. It does not change the fact that Mr. Shumway sacrificed his life for theirs and that they are saved. The family is saved and alive because and only because of Mr. Shumway. They did nothing, it was all him. So whether they follow rules or not, whether they believe or not, the truth is they are saved.

Neighbor four explained this salvation to family and when the family recognized this was indeed what happened, they lived the rest of their life in thanksgiving, appreciation and love for Mr. Shumway. Whether the family loved Shumway, forgot about him, live horrible lives or chose not to believe what he did, it does not change the fact that Mr. Shumway saved them. They are alive because of Mr. Shumway and the realization of this is what caused them to live in appreciation.

Well, you got it! Mr. Shumway in this story is Jesus Christ. Scripture says that Christ saves all humanity through His death and resurrection. He certainly did and that's the end of it. However, this is not what the pastors, priests and preachers of Christianity teach. They have the same teaching of the first two neighbors that try to convince the family that they need to do something in order to be saved when Shumway already guaranteed their safety. The neighbors minimized the work of Shumway because they put rules and actions on the family when their salvation was completely outside of themselves and all based on the actions of the neighbor who carried them out of the house. This is what religion does to Jesus Christ. Christ's death and resurrection will eventually save every man, woman and child that has ever, is currently, or will ever walk the face of this Earth. We as humans did nothing to accomplish this. We were like the family lying unconscious in the burning house. This story is an illustration to show that salvation is taken care of by Jesus; however, not everyone is saved at the moment. People will go through a process and even death before they enter the realization of salvation.

Virtually every religion in the world puts the decision and power on humans to believe, act right or perform certain rituals to reach God. The story of Christ Jesus is not a religion because He accomplishes one hundred percent of salvation for every human regardless of anything they do. Religion will try to make you act right to make you earn what you already have. Jesus paid the price in full for all. Watch how the following verses from scripture detail how death and justification are given to all humanity while not taking into consideration anything the human did or didn't do.

Consequently, then, as it was through one offense for all mankind for condemnation, thus also it is through one just reward for all mankind for life's justifying. For even as, through the disobedience of one man (Adam), the many were constituted sinners, thus also, through the obedience of the One (Jesus), the many shall be constituted just.
- Romans 5: 18-19

The 'all mankind' and the 'many' are in direct correlation to each other and these words mean everyone. Adam sinned before we were even born and yet this sin spread to all humanity. We had no choice in this. In the same way through Christ's obedience, justification spread to all humanity. We had no choice in this as well. Christians and religion will tell you that because of Adam's sin we all have fallen and are sinners. This is true. However, they will then say that what Jesus did only applies to us if we believe. That is not what this scripture says. We didn't need to believe in Adam in order for sin to apply to us. Therefore, we do not need to believe in Jesus in order for His obedience to apply to us. Religion wants to inject belief and acting right into these verses so that people need to check with the church to see if they are on the right track. The church is an unnecessary medium for justification. **Romans 5:20 says that where sin increases, grace superexceeds.** This means that the death and resurrection of Jesus Christ will overcome any sin. In essence, the more you sin, the greater the grace that covers that sin.

The following scripture confirms the message and relationship between Adam and Jesus Christ. Understand how the actions of these two individuals spread to all humans without consideration of what the human does or does not do.

For even as, in Adam, all are dying, thus also, in Christ, shall all be made alive.
- *1 Corinthians 15: 22*

This verse in Corinthians begins to set the table with respect to the order of people entering heaven. All people will be saved but those that are given belief will enter before the rest. This realization that Jesus Christ is the savior of the world, the entire world, without any human contribution is given by God to the believer. If you do not believe this, then God simply has not given you belief yet. However, the death and resurrection of Jesus Christ still applies to you. Adolf Hitler will be given life through Jesus Christ even though he may be the last one to enter. So here again, we have the above scripture in Paul's letter to the Corinthians saying that in Adam, all are dying. All humans begin to die as soon as they are born as each day inches closer to death. But, humans didn't choose this death although it applies to each and every one of us. We don't have to believe it or follow rules to achieve it. Death will find us no matter what we do or believe. That is Adam's contribution.

Right now, we have sin and death all around us. I'm sure that all of us have experienced enough of this in our lifetimes. If we look around, sin and death are running rampant. Children die every day because they don't have enough food, people are murdered exponentially, and the media glorifies every type of Godless act. We are living in the image of Adam. As mentioned before, some people seem better and more Godlike than others, but we all are in the flesh and all are subject to sin and death. We didn't ask for this, we were born into it. Not one of us could have been born and said, "I will reject sin and death and will live forever." It's not possible for a fleshly, descendant of Adam to accomplish this. We have taken on the likeness of Adam and Eve.

However, Adam is only the beginning not the end. Previously, I mentioned that evil serves a purpose. We must experience evil in order to have the knowledge of good and evil. This experience is the precursor to an amazing fulfillment that will be all the more enjoyed because of the present evil we have within us and outside of us. Again, we experience this because we were born into Adam. However, scripture says that as we were born in Adam and are like Adam, we will again be born into someone else and will be like that someone else. Who is that someone else? Just as everyone has taken on the likeness of Adam, everyone, and I mean everyone, will take on the likeness of this 'Someone else.' So, who is this someone else?

So it is written: The first Adam became a living being;" the last Adam, a life giving spirit (I Corinthians 15:45). This 'someone else' is the last Adam. **The first man was of the dust of the earth; the second man is of heaven (1 Corinthians 15:47).** The relationship between this 'last Adam' and 'second man' carry the same power than the original Adam, in the sense that all people will be like him. But I'll take it a step further. This last Adam and second man carry more power because he undoes, creates, or makes new all that the first Adam has touched. **And just as we have born the image of the earthly man** (Adam)**, so shall we bear the image of the heavenly man (1 Corinthians 15:49).**

Why, then, do we need to go through the process and bear the image of the first Adam? Part of the answer is in **1 Corinthians 15:46** that says: **The spiritual did not come first, but the natural, and after that the spiritual.** First, we have to pass through the evil, sin and death of the first Adam, in order to be born again into the last Adam, second man, heavenly man. Okay, so if you have not guessed it by now, that 'someone else,' last Adam, second man and heavenly man is Jesus Christ.

Jesus Christ did more than just die on the cross. **The Son is the image of the invisible God, the firstborn over all creation (Colossians 1:15).** Yes, by dying on the cross, Jesus assured that we will not remain dead and one day, will be resurrected. However, through death, Jesus also showed us what we will one day be. He showed us what we will be like when death is destroyed and sin has run its course and when both sin and death are destroyed. He showed us what we will be when we throw off the fleshly, natural first Adam. What will we one day be like, better yet, who did Jesus show us that we will one day be like? We will be like Him!

For those God foreknew He also predestined to be conformed to the image of His Son, that he might be the firstborn over many brothers and sisters (Romans 8:29).

Jesus Christ is the firstborn of a new creation. A creation that is resurrected and perfected to be the very sons of God. Jesus did this through death and resurrection, the same way He will do it in us. Adam was the firstborn of a creation that would eventually die. Everyone that is born becomes like Adam because of the sin and death operating in humanity. The reason Jesus is referred to as the second or last Adam is because He is the firstborn, like Adam, only of something new and better. Consequently, just as we are all born into Adam's sin, we will all be perfected through the death and resurrection of Jesus Christ. Again, **for as in Adam all die, so in Christ all will be made alive (1 Corinthians 15:22).** If death touches infants that have made no choice to sin but are born into a weak, death ridden humanity, then, the second Adam will impart His life in the same manner that the first Adam imparted his death to humanity. Therefore, through His death and resurrection, Jesus declares: **"I am making everything new"… (Revelation 21:5).**

This is God's glorious plan! Humanity will pass through decay and death in order to become a son of God, just like Jesus. Jesus was the first, He showed us the way and because of Him, all of us will pass from Adam's death to Christ's life. **For the creation was subjected to frustration, not by its own choice, but by the one who subjected it, in hope that the creation itself will be liberated from its bondage of decay and brought into the freedom and glory of the children of God (Romans 8:20-21).** This hope is God's destiny for all mankind.

Do you want to know God's purpose for us? It is to create billions of sons and daughters, though each one unique, that will have all of His attributes. Jesus Christ was the first and through Him, God will bring all humanity to be His precious sons and daughters. That is our destiny and that is what this life, this evil, this plan for the ages is all about.

The rest of the scripture says that in the same way Adam's death is spread to all people, in Christ, all people will be made alive. The phrase 'for even as' and 'thus also' are used to show that the action of Adam and Christ spread to people equally. Therefore, if we are given death by Adam with no action of our own then we are given life by Christ with no action of our own. Notice that the scripture in 1 Corinthians 15:22 does not say 'all in Christ will be made alive' but it says that '**in Christ, shall all be made alive.**' This applies to all people not just those that are in Christ right now. God saves some now and will save the rest later. Believers now are given a special salvation and they will work with Jesus in the ages to come in order to bring the rest of creation to Jesus Christ.

God, Who is the Savior of all mankind, especially of believers (1 Timothy 4:10).

God will save everybody. Believers have a special salvation of coming in to the plan early and ruling and reigning with Christ in the ages to come. However, the 'especially' qualifies the rest as also being saved. So in conclusion, Jesus either saved us or He didn't. The bible says that He did and this is a fact! A person's belief or actions does not change this fact. Belief gives us a realization of the truth but does not make it true.

CHAPTER 9

GOD WILL BE ALL THINGS TO ALL PEOPLE—EVERY LAST HUMAN WILL BE SAVED

Okay, now back to the scripture that proves one day sin and death will be destroyed or rendered inoperative. **1 Corinthians 15: 22-28** might be my favorite group of verses in all of scripture. It describes the whole plan in only seven verses. Verse 22 starts with the comparison of Adam and Christ which I have already discussed in some detail. But to review, this verse tells that all will die because of Adam. We can see this because people die and we know that one day we will die. However, the second part of this verse is something we don't quite see yet. The same "all" used to describe those Adam touches is the same "all" that is used to describe those who will be made alive through Christ. Notice that this verse does not say that "all" in Christ will be made alive but in Christ, "all" will be made alive. That's everyone! Now, there are some other interesting things about the rest of the verses in this set of scripture:

For as in Adam all die, so in Christ all will be made alive But each in his own turn: Christ, the firstfruits; then, when he comes, those who belong to him. Then the end will come, when he hands over the kingdom to God the Father after he has destroyed all dominion, authority and power. For he must reign until he has put all his enemies under his feet. The last enemy to be destroyed is death. For he "has put everything under his feet." Now when it says that "everything" has been put under him, it is clear that this does not include God himself, who put everything under Christ. When he has done this, then the Son himself will be made subject to him who put everything under him, so that God may be all in all. – 1 Corinthians 15: 22 – 28

In the end, Jesus will destroy all things by reconciling them to God. **For in Him all things were created: things in heaven and on earth, visible and invisible, whether thrones or powers or rulers or authorities; all things have been created through him and for him (Colossians 1:16)… and through him to reconcile to himself all things, whether things on earth or things in heaven, by making peace through his blood, shed on the cross (Colossians 1:20).**

You see, all things were created for Christ. Even the evil things and powers we see in the world today. However, those things will be put under Jesus' feet because of the cross. The last thing the Lord will put under his feet is death. He will destroy death. The Greek word used for 'destroy' in this verse actually means 'to render inoperative, abolish.' So, death will be inoperative or abolished at God's chosen time. Therefore, if death is destroyed all that is left is life. People cannot remain dead if death is abolished or no longer operating. This refutes the claims made by those who believe that the wicked would cease to exist (annihilation). However, I believe death being destroyed goes a step further. The book of Revelation talks about the second death. Many people in the church contend that this 'second death' is eternal hell. In essence, all the unsaved are cast into the lake of fire and this is the second death. My question is: what happens to the people in the lake of fire, experiencing the second death, when death is destroyed?

The answer is that those in the lake of fire will eventually have life as well, eternal life. Death will be inoperative, abolished. First death, second death, it does not matter. Death will be destroyed so that it no longer has any hold on God's creation. If people are imprisoned to some eternal hell, then the second death has a hold on them. This is not possible since death has been annulled. Therefore, this refutes the claim of those that believe people are in eternal hell.

Now, I am not saying that people will not be judged. We will all be judged and it starts in the house of God as scripture proclaims. This judgment will be experienced by believers first and unbelievers in a more intense form, later. However, this judgment will be for the benefit of the one being judged. Through judgment, we all learn righteousness. So, the person that makes the argument: "Well then, if there is no hell than I can kill, cheat and steal." Yes, Jesus died for all sin and that person will have everlasting life but will not be saved until they pass through judgment to learn righteousness. **When your judgments come upon the earth, the people of the world learn righteousness (Isaiah 26:9).**

The Greatest Words of All

The last eight words in **1 Corinthians 15:28** are probably my most cherished of all words in scripture. It tells us what this experience of life is all about and why we go through evil and all other things. These words tell us what God's end goal is for all humanity. You see, there will come a time when Jesus puts everything under Him, all of God's creation, under himself. At this point, Jesus will cease to reign and will be made subject to Almighty God. Jesus only does this when He has finished or accomplished what He set out to do on the cross. Jesus is made subject to God once he has saved all of God's creation.

Now, here are the words, the end goal for God and our own destiny. Why do we experience what we experience as humans? Why did Jesus do what He did?

...so that God can be all in all (1 Corinthians 15:28). God will be all in all of his creation. There is no room for evil, sin or death at this point. All of that nonsense served its purpose and now has been annulled or is no longer operating, destroyed! God cannot be all in all if in some distant corner of the universe or alternate dimension, sin and death still reined in eternal hell. If God is all in all, then all humans have the image of God and are truly sons of God. This is our glorious destiny. God is all in all people. The following six steps outline and review God's plan to save all mankind.

STEP 1: <u>**For as in Adam all die, even so in Christ all shall be made alive.**</u>

This sentence, like hundreds of others in scripture destroys the demonic doctrine of eternal hell and human free will. Adam sinned against God and because of that all creation dies. We did not have a free will choice in the matter, what Adam did was imparted to every single human being before we are even born. But this is the good news; Jesus Christ imparts life to every single human being just as Adam imparted death. This means that Christ gives life to the same all in which Adam gave death. EVERY SINGLE PERSON. Again, we have no free choice in the matter. This verse does not say, as Christians would tell you, for as in Adam all die but only those who believe in Christ shall be made alive. NO, lying pastors, it doesn't say that! The same all that is touched by Adam's death are touched by Christ's resurrection!

I guess Adam's action was more powerful than Christ's. Religion and Christians would have you believe that. It is simply not true. God's plan was to have His only begotten son, Jesus, die on the cross. This was the plan from creation, before Adam even sinned. **….The Lamb Who was slain from the creation of the world (Revelations 13:8).** God's plan is that all people die through Adam and all people are made alive Through Jesus Christ. The cross was not an afterthought or part of God's damage control to save as many people as He could after Adam sinned. No, the cross and Adam's sin were always a part of God's plan. God chose to create sons and daughters by using sin, death and Jesus.

God was not left to wonder what to do after Adam sinned, Adam's sin and the cross of Jesus Christ were part of the plan from the beginning. God created the problem and provided the solution to prepare us for the greatest possible eternal joy. The cross is plan A, not plan B.

STEP 2: But each in his own order: Christ the firstfruits, afterward those who are Christ's at His coming.

Believers do have a special salvation. Those who are chosen by God to come to the realization that Christ alone saves them will be saved before those who were not given belief in this life. Christ has been resurrected first, the next group to be resurrected is those who died believing in Jesus and who are living believers when Jesus Christ returns. The living believers when Christ returns are the only ones that don't experience death before they are made immortal.

…God, Who is the Saviour of all mankind, especially of believers (1 Timothy 4:10). This verse speaks of the special salvation of believers, but, it qualifies non-believers of being saved by God as well. You see, God saves all mankind, but has a special chosen place for those who believe. So, what about those who do not believe?

STEP 3: Then comes the end, when He delivers the kingdom to God the Father, when He puts an end to all rule and all authority and power.

The next phase of God's plan is to end all rule, authority and power. What are these exactly? **Ephesians 6:12** says, **For we do not wrestle** against flesh and blood, but against <u>principlaties, against powers,</u> <u>against the rulers of the darkness of this age, against spiritual hosts</u> <u>of wickedness in the heavenly places.</u> First, we need to understand that the apostle Paul, in this verse, is speaking of wickedness in the heavenly realms. These spiritual hosts are not in hell but in the heavenly realms. This rule, authority and power are pure evil. We are talking demons, Satan here. God says that Jesus puts an end to this entire evil rule, evil authority that the devil and his demons have, and all the evil power. How does Jesus end this evil dominion? That question is answered in **Colossians.**

And by Him (Jesus) to reconcile all things to Himself, by Him, whether things on earth or things in <u>Heaven</u> having made peace through the blood of the cross. Earlier in **Colossians 16,** it says, **For by Him (Jesus) all things were created that are in heaven and that are on the earth, visible and invisible, whether thrones or dominions or principalities or powers. All things were created through Him and for Him.**

Okay, now I'm quoting scripture like a Baptist preacher. What does this all mean? It means that God created all evil, demons and Satan himself and once they have served their purpose, God ends their rule, power and authority by making peace through the blood of Jesus Christ. Don't worry, extreme judgement awaits these evil doers, however, in the end, Jesus Christ brings all of God's creation under the subjugation of God. That is how he puts an end to all rule, power and authority.

STEP 4: For He must reign till He has put all enemies under His feet. The last enemy to be destroyed is death.

Jesus prayed to God to forgive those killing Him, He will save all sinners and enemies by reconciling them to God. The last enemy to be destroyed is death. Let's notice two things about the sentences above that are not taught in bible studies or Sunday school. How many times have you heard your pastor teach about the fact that Jesus Christ's reign will end? I'm thinking rarely if ever. However, scripture clearly says that the Lord's reign will end. When? Not until the last enemy is destroyed. Through Adam came death and we all die. Jesus Christ will reign until He destroys death. At this point, there is only life, eternal life for all people. Death is not operating at all, it is destroyed. People are not experiencing eternal death (annihilationism) or any type of ridiculous, ludicrous, sick eternal hell. All sin, death and evil have been done away with at this point.

You see Christians have it all wrong. Jesus didn't die on the cross and rise from the dead and then try to get as many followers as possible. He died on the cross and rose from the dead to save everybody. God works out the individual details in each and everyone's life as far as timing, belief and that kind of stuff.

Imagine for a second, that there was a mighty cruise ship waiting at the dock and its destination was a beautiful paradise across the ocean. If you got on the ship, you went to the beautiful paradise. If you didn't get on the ship than the place you were at was going to get hit by a hurricane and everything would be destroyed. According to Christianity, Jesus Christ would run to the ship and then try to call out or get his friends to tell as many people as possible to get on the ship before it leaves. Jesus is on the boat, others follow, but now the boat is leaving and many were left behind to die in the coming hurricane. That is not the loving savior scenario. The truth is that Jesus will tell people about the ship and have others do the same. Then Jesus stands outside the ship and does not board until the last, the very last person on the island gets in the boat. When every last one of the people on the island are on that ship that is when Jesus boards. This is the meaning of these verses. Jesus saved everyone, now everyone is reconciled and subject to God. Now Jesus steps in to be subjugated to God and gives up His reign. Mission accomplished, saved the entire creation, minus not one living thing.

STEP 5: For "He has put all things under His feet." But when He says "all things are put under Him," it is evident that He who put all things under Him is excepted.

Absolutely everything is reconciled to God by Jesus Christ. The only thing that is not reconciled to God by Jesus is God Himself. The scriptures specifically say this, if other creation, people, or entities were not reconciled to God, then they would be mentioned here. But no, God is the only one Who is not subject to Jesus Christ.

Now I want to be clear that we are saved by grace through faith. Even the vilest evil is ordained by God to serve a good purpose. However, people will be judged by God and it will not be pleasant. But, judgement is not eternal and in the end, is corrective.

STEP 6: Now when all things are made subject to Him, then the Son Himself will also be subject to Him who put all things under Him, So that God may be all in all.

I made the last eight words in this verse very big because those words sum up the destiny of every single person and the reason for Sin, death, judgement, resurrection, Jesus Christ, and all that there is. This is God's end game, His grand intention. God will be all things in all people. We will have gone through sin, evil and death so we will know, like God, just how wonderful things are at this point, because we went through all the pain.

One of the main reasons that people do not understand the bible correctly is because of the mistranslation of the Greek word aion, aionios. It has been translated in many bibles to mean eternity, when in fact, the word actually means eon or eons, denoting a period of time that has a beginning and an end.

God has a plan for the ages/eons. The present eon we are in now is coming to a close. The future eons or ages that the bible speaks of are Christ's Millennium Reign and New Heavens and New Earth. Those of us that believe that Jesus Christ's death and His death alone on the cross was 100% sufficient for humanity's salvation; these people will be alive during these two glorious ages. Those who do not believe in Jesus or add something to the cross, like their own free will choice, faith in themselves, faith in their faith or trust in any type of work will be resurrected at a later time. Those that have faith in Jesus Christ, a belief of pure grace, are those that enjoy this special salvation. At the consummation, the end of the ages, all people, all the dead, will be raised to life with God when death is destroyed. So again, and I am repeating this because so few understand these truths, Jesus saved every single human that has ever or will ever walk the face of the earth, on the cross. However, God gives faith to people at different times. Faith is a realization that Jesus died for you and you had nothing to do at all, with your salvation. Your salvation and life's blueprint was sealed for you just as death was imparted to you.

I understand that Jesus doing all the work for us is a very difficult concept to grasp. After all, children are rewarded and punished for their actions at a very young age. Teachers create entire behavior systems based on rewarding good behavior and punishing bad behavior. Prisons are built for those who make bad choices. **SORRY,** God's ways are not our ways and the cross of Jesus Christ does not operate that way. God did not create a behavior system, He sent His Son. Jesus Christ completed the task; our systems are useless when it comes to salvation. All of our failures and sins were put on Jesus at the cross, not on a behavior chart. In fact, the behavior chart was completely eliminated because God sees us, behavior wise, as He sees His Son Jesus. If we still want to use the behavior chart or add any works, then we have to be perfect and keep the entire law. Good luck.

Love your Enemies

Christians say that Jesus Christ is the only way to get to heaven. I believe this one-hundred percent, however, my belief differs from Christianity because I believe the cross is for all mankind and all eventually find their way home through the cross. This process is all of God.

Do you remember what Jesus said about the people who were killing him while he was on the cross? He said a prayer to his father. Jesus said, **"Father, forgive them, for they know not what they are doing (Luke 23:34)."** Think about this, Jesus was asking forgiveness for those who were taunting him, spitting at him, and nailing him to the cross. These people were nowhere in the ballpark of making a personal confession for Jesus Christ. They were killing the Son of God. Yet, Jesus asked for their forgiveness. Do you believe the father denied the Lord's request? No way! The Jews and Romans that were crucifying Christ were performing what God had ordained them to perform since the beginning of creation. The Son had to go to the cross to save humanity. Therefore, the world's worst evil became the greatest good because the cross will save all mankind. Did God will it this way or does God actually will people to act in seemingly bad ways? **Indeed Herod and Pontius Pilate met together with the Gentiles and the people of Israel in this city to conspire against your holy servant**

Jesus, whom you appointed. They (Pilate and Herod) did what your power and will (God's) had decided beforehand should happen (Acts 4: 27-28). God decided beforehand, before Pilate and Herod had any say so, to use these men to bring Jesus to the cross. It was God's will, not Herod's, Pilate's, or any other human beings free will choice. No, it was God's will to use these men to conspire and eventually bring Jesus to the cross.

Anyway, back to Jesus forgiving his murderers. If these men were forgiven, then that means God can forgive those who have not chosen Jesus, as this account clearly shows these men despised Jesus. I seriously don't believe that any Christian denies the fact that God granted Jesus' request to forgive these men. Therefore, I think it is safe to say that Jesus will forgive us for lesser sins and overcome these sins, even the sin of unbelief. We will all believe eventually and in God's timing.

Religion paints the picture of a dual, conditional and schizophrenic god. He loves you only if you love him. Yes, Christians and other religions sing and talk of God's love but what they preach is not love at all. They teach that Jesus died for you but that was not enough. The individual must do something to activate or accept Jesus Christ. Jesus loves you but if you don't love him then God will burn you for all eternity. In addition, the invitation only extends until your life is over. If you don't accept Jesus before you die then God's love ends. How can anyone trust in a love or a God like that? I can't imagine anymore, though I once did, believing in a God that will love me only if I do certain things for Him. That means that my salvation is up to me and I would always have to be concerned about myself. This takes the saving power away from Jesus and puts it on me. So, in conclusion, it will always be possible that Jesus will turn His back on me if I don't toe the line.

Thank God that salvation is a sure thing and God's love never runs out and Jesus does not turn His back on anyone. Scripture says that Jesus saved me and it is a sure thing. In fact, His death applies to me even if I hated Him and was a complete and total enemy of God. **For if, being enemies, we were conciliated to God through the death of His Son, much rather, being conciliated, we shall be saved in His life (Romans 5: 10-11).** These verses speak of God making humans right with Him WHILE THEY ARE HIS ENEMIES! You see, God saves you and loves you even when you reject him. Jesus's death on the cross covers all sin, even the sin of unbelief. It does not matter how far you drift from God or what you have or have not done in your life because salvation is not up to you. Salvation is the work of Jesus Christ and **we are His achievement (Ephesians 2:10).** While we were enemies, Jesus made us right with God. He does not wait until we accept Him or follows rules to show our loyalty. God saves us and loves us at our worst and there is nothing we can do to make Him stop loving us. Now that is a God I can trust in and that is the God of the bible.

The next words of Jesus that I am going to discuss are kind of a rallying cry for Christians, but I am not sure how it is practiced. In **Matthew, chapter 5**, Jesus instructs the crowds to love their enemies and pray for those who persecute them. In **Luke 6:35**, it says Jesus instructed the crowds to love their enemies and do good to them. That is a hard thing to do as I think we could all agree. I find it hard enough to love those close to me the way I should, as opposed to actually loving my enemies. But, what does Jesus mean by loving our enemies? Well, it means showing them love and caring for them, right? So I ask another question, how does the doctrine of an eternal hell show love for the people that are there?

Supposedly, according to Christianity, people who reject Christ will spend an eternity in hell. Well, these people would classify as being God's enemies, don't you think? Wait a minute, Jesus instructed us to love our enemies. Does any one of us truly believe that torturing a human being in unimaginable pain, flesh ripping locusts and flames engulfing a screaming being, horrors beyond imagination, actually shows love to that person? Not to mention that this will go on not for a million years, but all eternity, forever. Also, that this torture serves no purpose because the person in hell will never actually get better or be refined. All of God's judgments are designed to make people better or draw them towards Him. Like any child properly disciplined…**When your judgments come upon the earth, the people of the world learn righteousness (Isaiah 26:9).** God's judgment, though fierce, corrects and is for the benefit of the person being judged. Judgment flows from God's mercy and is not designed to satisfy God as an end in itself.

Now, all Christians will stand at once and tell me that it was their choice to reject Jesus and they chose to go to hell (like anyone would make a free will choice to go to such a place). But let's say that is true, that makes them God's enemies. Again, Jesus instructs us to love our enemies. Is God asking us to do something that He won't do? He is if we believe in an eternal hell. God is torturing his enemies while we are instructed to love ours or worse yet, is letting his enemies be tortured and doing nothing about it. Either way, God does not love his enemies and the process doesn't make any sense. The truth is that God does love his enemies. He proves this in **Romans, Chapter 5**. God sent his son to die for his enemies and one day God will bring all of his enemies under subjugation to Christ (**I Corinthians 15:25**) and will bring them all home to heaven. That is love!

CHAPTER 10

THE PROCESS OF SALVATION (GRACE AND FAITH)

In Christian circles, everyone seems to have a formula for salvation that each person needs to follow. Some believe that you need to be baptized in order to be saved, some believe you need to follow a certain set of rules, some believe you need to complete certain sacraments, some believe you only need to believe in Jesus by choosing Him of your own volition, etc., etc., etc.

Christianity alone teaches many different routes to salvation. That's not to mention the hundreds of other religions in the world that have their own views on the process of salvation. So, how can we possible know how we are saved? Well, the scriptural answer is that we are saved by grace!

The word "Grace" is revealing because this very word means that it is something that we do not deserve or have not earned. Strong's concordance defines grace as divine influence on the heart. The Concordant Literal defines grace as a benefit bestowed on one who deserves the opposite. By these definitions, grace is given to humans from God undeservedly and with influence. As a result, it can be concluded that people are influenced by God through grace which eliminates the possibility of free-will and human determination. It is all of God.

We do not obtain grace from baptism, good works or any other human action. Otherwise, grace would cease to be grace. Okay, how do we receive grace one might ask? You receive the gift of grace through faith! Faith is the vehicle that God uses to distribute grace. However, and this is what the church does not understand, faith is a gift from God. People do not make a free will choice or get faith from any outside source. God simply distributes a measure of faith to each individual by which He imparts grace. Grace does not necessarily mean that we do nothing, but it means we do nothing apart from God. **Titus 2:11** says that grace is used to train us to live in a Godly way. **Ephesians 2:10** says that **we, being created in Christ Jesus for good works, which God makes ready beforehand, that we should be walking in them.** So, we are saved purely by the death and resurrection of Jesus Christ but that does not mean that we are not trained to do good works or to walk in them. These good works are predestined for us to do through the grace freely given to us by God. We do not do them on our own or out of our supposed free-will.

I sometimes hear arguments that if everyone is saved then humans can do whatever they want. They can lie, steal, cheat and kill and still be saved. This is misguided thinking. Yes, all people will eventually be saved. But, the grace of God operating in you will teach people to become like Jesus Christ. Some will go through this process now and others later. However, no human will enter the kingdom as a liar, cheater and murderer.

For it is by grace you have been saved, through faith – and this is not of yourselves, it is the gift of God (Ephesians 2:8). God saves people by His grace by giving them faith to believe in Jesus Christ. People don't get faith from a tent revival, they get it from God. That's not to say that God doesn't use people to bring his message to others, but, it does mean that God chooses who will accept the message. **For by the grace given me I say to every one of you: Do not think of yourself more highly than you ought, but rather think of yourself with sober judgment, in accordance with the faith God has distributed to each of you (Romans 12:3).** Other translations say: in accordance with the measure of faith God has given you. Bottom line, we need faith in order to get grace, but this faith comes directly from God.

Okay, so we will be saved by grace through faith. Saved from what? We will be saved from many different things, such as sin, weakness, the flesh, ourselves, Satan, etc. However, the deepest part of the cross has to do with bringing life from death. Please pay special attention to this verse in **1 Corinthians 15:22: For as in Adam all die, so in Christ all will be made alive.** Adam's sin has been passed down to all humans and all of creation. Do you want to know what has been affected by Adam's sin? Everything that dies is affected by Adam's sin. **For as is Adam all die,** means that we have death operating in us until we breathe our last breath. Sin, also, is closely related to death and is a part of us as well. It wasn't our choice, through the actions of Adam; we were all touched by sin and death. **For the creation was subject to frustration, not by its own choice, but by the will of the one who subjected it, in hope that the creation itself will be liberated from its bondage to decay and brought into the freedom and glory of the children of God (Romans 8:20-21).**

The second part of the **1 Corinthians 15:22** contains some of the most fascinating and exciting words in scripture. **So in Christ all will be made alive.** This is parallel language. Everything that Adam has touched with death, will also be made alive in Christ. The scripture does not say that only those who are in Christ or those who believe in Christ will be made alive. No, it says that **in Christ all will be made alive.** All of what Adam touched with sin and death will be made alive by Christ. Remember, if you want to know what has been touched by Adam and sin then look at everything that dies. Dogs, ducks, deer and especially humans all die. All creation has been subjected to this decay and frustration, not by its choice, but by God (Romans 8: 20-21). Why? So that in Christ we will be made alive.

Do you want to know who Jesus will save? Do you want to know who eventually will be with God? Do you want to know if Jesus will save all mankind? The answer, from **1 Corinthians 15:22,** is that anything that has been touched by death will be made alive by Christ. If it dies, it will be made alive.

Consequently, just as one trespass resulted in condemnation for all people, so also one righteous act resulted in justification and life for all people (Romans 5:18). The trespass of Adam brought condemnation for every single one of us. No one could escape this condemnation; otherwise, they would not be subject to death. If someone you know lived a near perfect life, would they be free from death? No, death is imparted to us all. Remember, trees and dogs die as well. They are not even capable of sinning. And yet, death touches them as well. However, the one righteous act of Christ resulted in justification and life for all people that are subject to this condemnation. That means life for all people. Jesus will one day lift the curse off this earth.

Religious people who believe that sin and death will keep multitudes of people in some sort of hellish torment for all eternity; do not pay attention to these scriptures. Adam's sin has spread to all humanity and the proof of this is that we all die. We cannot make a choice not to die, we will one day die. So Adam is very powerful in the fact that his act spread to all people. Now, Christ committed an act as well. The scripture says that this righteous act spread to all people as well. However, many Christians want to say that Adam's sin spread to all humanity but Christ's righteous act only spreads to a precious few. This is not true. Everything that has been touched by death will be made alive by Christ. Adam's act resulted in condemnation for ALL PEOPLE! Jesus' righteous act resulted in justification and life for ALL PEOPLE! Please ponder **1 Corinthians 15:22 and Romans 5:18.** Please throw away tradition and any pre-conceived ideas and just see what these verses actually say.

If Adam's sin has touched all people and Jesus' death and resurrection is limited to only a few, then it would be safe to say that Adam's sin is more powerful than the cross. It would say that Adam's sin and death are so powerful that in touches all humans without choice. Whereas, Christ's death and resurrection are so weak that they do not spread to all humanity. However, **Romans 5:20** says …**But where sin increased, grace increased all the more…**How could this be unless the grace of Jesus Christ saved all those who have sinned.

Okay, my point is this: If because of Adam's sin, sin spread to all creation, then in order for the cross of Christ to be greater than sin, the salvation of the cross would have to at least spread to all creation to be as powerful as sin. Therefore, we, without a choice, have been subjected to sin and death, and this has an impact on everyone. If the cross of Christ only saved a few that have managed to believe in this lifetime, then sin has taken more of creation than the cross was able to save. So we conclude that sin is greater and more powerful than the cross. But, our hearts, **Romans 5:20** and countless other scriptures say that this is not true. **So that, just as sin reigned in death, so also grace might reign through righteousness to bring eternal life through Jesus Christ our Lord (Romans 5:21).** Christians attempt to get God off the hook by free-will. That is simply not how God has set things up. He does not need people to get Him off the hook, His plan will save all.

CHAPTER 11

GOD'S PLAN FOR THE AGES

God has a magnificent, wonderful plan for humanity. This plan, once the ages of time run their course, ends with God being **ALL IN ALL: PERFECTING EVERY MAN, WOMAN, CHILD AND CREATURE THAT HE CREATED!** However, a process of time and ages must pass in order for this plan to become complete. FIRST, let's begin with who God put in charge of creating His creatures and the one in charge of completing the process of perfection: *SPOILER ALERT—IT IS HIS SON, JESUS CHRIST!*

Who is the Image of the invisible God, Firstborn of every creature, for in Him is all created, that in the heavens and that on the earth, the visible and the invisible, whether thrones, or lordships, or sovereignties, or authorities, all is created through Him and for Him, and He is before All, and all has its cohesion in Him.

And He is the Head of the body, the ecclesia, Who is Sovereign, Firstborn from among the dead, that in all He may becoming first, for in Him the entire complement delights to dwell, and through Him to reconcile all to Him (making peace through the blood of His cross), through Him, whether those on earth or those in the heavens.
  - *Colossians 1: 15-20*

These verses clearly explain that through Jesus Christ all was created and that through Jesus Christ, all will be reconciled by Jesus Christ. These verses are amazing because an explanation is given about the entire creation and the one responsible for this creation. If that wasn't enough, these verses explain exactly what creation is. Paul, in this letter to the Colossians, tells that through Jesus, <u>all</u> was created and <u>all</u> will be reconciled. Then, goes on to explain exactly what this <u>ALL</u> includes.

Soooooooooo.........scripture says that all was created and all will be reconciled by Jesus. Does this mean that everyone that has ever walked the face of the earth will be with God in the end? That kind of goes against the teachings of every religion in the world. Well, the TRUTH always goes against what religion teaches. Let's look at the 'ALL' described in these verses. Colossians says that Jesus **is the image of the invisible God, <u>Firstborn of every creature</u>, <u>for in Him is all created.</u>** What does every creature and all really include? This is answered immediately if you continue reading this passage. Paul continues to describe the ALL as *that in the heavens and that on the earth, the visible and the invisible, whether thrones, or lordships, or sovereignties, or authorities.* Okay, let's divert to Ephesians 6:12 now to settle what exactly this means:

...For it is not ours to wrestle with blood and flesh, but with the sovereignties, with the authorities, with the world-mights of this darkness, with the spiritual forces of wickedness among the celestials.
  - Ephesians 6:12

Paul explains that not only did God create all humanity and benevolent beings through Jesus Christ, but He also created Satan, demons, and all wicked things whether seen or unseen. He created evil and the beings that will carry this evil out. In fact, evil and good exist together in the order and relationship that God has determined as they **have cohesion in Jesus Christ.** Now, please notice that these wicked creations are in heaven, as scripture says these **spiritual forces are among the celestials.** They are not contained in hell which is a clearly fictitious teaching if scriptures are translated properly.

NOW HERE'S THE KIKKER: Scripture says that all of creation, including the wicked, will be reconciled to God through Jesus Christ! *Through Him to reconcile all to Him (making peace through the blood of His cross), through Him, whether those on earth or those in the heavens.* So, Colossians 1:15-20 actually says that through Jesus all was created. Then, goes on to explain exactly what that all is: All people, spiritual entities, animals and everything else. Then, when it is all said and done, Jesus will reconcile all to God. That means that every man, women, child, spirit, animal, demon, and yes, even Satan will be reconciled to God. However, each in their own order. This order is explained in the New Testament letter to the Corinthians:

For even as, in Adam, all are dying, thus also, in Christ, shall all be made alive. Yet each in his own class: the Firstfruit, Christ; thereupon

those who are Christ's in His presence; thereafter the consummation,
whenever He may be giving up the kingdom to his God and Father,
whenever He should be nullifying all sovereignty and all authority
and power. For He must be reigning until He should be placing all
His enemies under His feet. The last enemy is being abolished: death.
For He subjects all under His feet. Now whenever He may be saying
that all is subject, it is evident that it is outside of Him Who subjects
all to Him. Now, whenever all may be subjected to Him, then the Son
Himself also shall be subjected to Him Who subjects all to Him, that
God may be All in All.

- *1 Corinthians 15: 22-28*

So **1 timothy 4:10** says that God will save all men, especially those who believe. The word especially means that believers will come in to everlasting life before unbelievers and enjoy ages of glory while others remain dead. However, Jesus will save the rest at a later time. Let's breakdown this order in the scriptures from Corinthians:

Before the order is announced, verse 22 says that **in Adam, all are dying, thus also in Christ, shall all be made alive.** Notice that this verse says that in Adam, all die and in Christ, all shall be made alive. It does not say that only those in Christ will be made alive, it says because of Christ, all will be made alive. That is a big difference! Christians want to mar this sentence by implying that only a select few will have Christ's accomplishment apply to them. However, these words clearly mean that through Christ, all creation will be made alive. We all know that because of Adam's sin, death spreads to all humanity. We have no choice in the matter; it applies to all humans without any action of our own. No human is immortal! In the same way, Christ's death and resurrection applies to all humans without any action of our own. Every human will one day put on immortality when Jesus makes them alive. Some will have this life before others. It is important to understand that salvation is for all and completely apart from any human effort or belief. Therefore, the question is never if a person will be saved and given new life but instead, when a person will be saved and given new life. Those that God chooses to give faith will be saved first; the rest will be saved later. So now, the order by which this will happen:

This first letter to the Corinthians lays out the plan and end game for God, through His Son, to reconcile all creation. However, this process is not completed over night. It takes the fullness of time (all ages) for Christ's death and resurrection to apply to all of creation. Believers, those that God has given the grace to believe the truth, will be resurrected at Christ's return to enjoy the 1,000 year (Millennial reign of Christ) kingdom. Unbelievers will remain in the dead state for this period of time. The bible says that the dead **know nothing** while they are dead. They are in a state of sleep, unconscious and unaware of any sensations or passage of time. They are not in hell or in any other fairy tale place, they are dead.

Then, after the 1,000 year kingdom ends, the believers that enjoyed the 1,000 years will take their immortality into the next age of time, the new heavens and the new earth. We do not know how long this lasts. After the 1,000 years, the dead unbelievers will be raised to face the Great White Throne Judgement. *The rest of the dead do not live until the thousand years should be finished (Revelations 20:5).* The following scripture in revelations describes the climate at the Great White Throne:

And I perceived a great white throne, and Him Who is sitting upon it, from Whose face earth and heaven fled, and no place was found for them.

And I perceived the dead, the great and the small, standing before the throne. And scrolls were opened. And another scroll was opened which is the scroll of life. And the dead were judged by that which is written in the scrolls in accord with their acts.

And the sea gives up the dead in it, and death and the unseen give up the dead in them. And they were condemned, each in accord with their acts. And death and the unseen were cast into the lake of fire. This is the second death – the lake of fire. And if anyone was not found written in the scroll of life, he was cast into the lake of fire.
- *Revelations 20: 11-15*

The people at the Great White Throne are being judged. Remember, scripture teaches that judgement is corrective and for the benefit of the person being judged. ***When your judgements come upon the earth, the people of the world learn righteousness (Isaiah 26:9).*** During this judgement, people that did not accept what Jesus did as their full justification, will be judged according to their acts, their good deeds and their evil ones. I don't know how long this judgement takes but God will correct each individual. I'm sure some will take longer than others. These people rejected the full sacrifice of Jesus Christ to cover their sins and now rely on their acts in front of the Almighty God. All people fall short without Christ Jesus and will be corrected at the Great White Throne. However, once corrected, these people will experience the second death or lake of fire as it is not their time to live. Again, no sensation will be felt by these people while in the death state. They will not feel a passage of time; they will be asleep until they are raised at the consummation. It will feel like an instant but these people will be dead during the new heavens and the new earth.

Now, I am not sure, based on individual judgement, whether some people will come out of the death state and enjoy some of the new heavens and the new earth, but, it is my understanding that these people will be dead until the consummation or the end of the ages. At the consummation, as Corinthians states, death will be destroyed and all will be made alive as the bible proclaims God will be all in all.

Basically, those that are given belief by God are given immortality early, before the rest. Why do some people get in early and given the faith and grace to believe? Simply, God decided and predestined certain people for this purpose. Others, He did not. These people did nothing of themselves to earn this, it is all of God and He is sovereign. This does not mean that God loves the chosen people more than others as we have no idea what it will be like when individual people are raised at the consummation. I believe God puts together the greatest, unimaginable plan of redemption for each individual during the consummation just like that of the chosen believers. There will be no spoiled brats in heaven; we will all have gone through the ringer of sin and death. In the end, unending glory with God for every single man, woman and child that has ever walked the face of the earth.

THE FIRSTFRUIT (1 CORINTHIANS 15:23)
Jesus is the first one to be raised from the dead to live beyond the reach of death.
1. THOSE WHO ARE CHRIST'S IN HIS PRESENCE (1 CORINTHIANS 15: 23)
The next group to be raised is those believers in Jesus that have died as well as those still alive during His return (1 Thessalonians 4: 13 -18). This includes those that have come to a realization that Christ Jesus accomplished 100% of salvation on the cross.
2. THE REST OF HUMANITY, CONSUMMATION (1 CORINTHIANS 15: 24)
All those that did not believe will be made alive when Jesus destroys death after the 1,000 year kingdom and the new heavens and the new earth. Everyone will enjoy being with God for all eternity at this point.

Therefore, the summary of God's complete plan for the ages. *For even as, in Adam, all are dying, thus also, in Christ shall all be made alive (1 Corinthians 15:22).* Adam›s sin and death spread to all humanity and humanity has no choice in the matter. In the same way as scripture declares, Christ›s death and resurrection spread to all humanity and humanity had no choice in the matter. Consequently, then, as it was through one offense for all mankind for condemnation, thus also it is through one just award for all mankind for life›s justification. *For even as, through the disobedience of the one man, the many were constituted sinners, thus also, through the obedience of the One, the many shall be constituted just (Romans 5: 18-19).* All humanity will be given salvation and live forever with God. Now on to the order presented in *1 Corinthians 15: 23-28:* Jesus was the first, believers will come next, and the consummation will end the ages and destroy death. At this point, all are alive and with God enjoying eternal bliss as God will be all in all!!! CHRIST WILL SAVE ALL THAT ADAM LOST: FOR CHRIST IS GREATER THAN ADAM!

Where sin increases, grace superexceeds (Romans 5:20).

God uses the fullness of time and the ages to accomplish His ultimate intention and purpose. We cannot fully understand the wisdom of God and why He chose to make evil, sin and death a necessary part of our creative process. However, we can trust the true God of scripture uses everything about us; every pain, every experience, every mistake, every circumstance, every person in our lives and every intimate part of our being is used to prepare us for an everlasting life that makes our heart throb with joy. There is nothing you or anyone else can do to ruin this eternal destiny because it is based on Christ's work and not yours. God will fill every creature with His Glory!

ABOUT THE AUTHOR

S.E. Hicko grew up in the Catholic Church and later ventured out to other mainstream Christian denominations. He is a special education teacher and his qualifications for writing this book do not come from church schools or institutions but from detailed personal study of scripture in its original meaning. He has listened to pastors and preachers and realizes they do not know the truth about God and His Son, Christ Jesus. He has found that the church clings to tradition and formalized, false ideas. Hicko has failed more than he has succeeded and relies on the finished work of His Savior as his only hope. Paul was a tentmaker, Peter was a fisherman, and Mary Magdalene was an outcast. These people needed the truth and they had to leave church institutions to find it. This author's only qualification is a personal, relentless pursuit of the truth that God loves enough to save all mankind and has devised a plan that will do exactly that.

Printed in the United States
By Bookmasters